Downton Abbey
on
Location

J. P. Sperati
&
Sabine Schreiner

All correspondence for
Downton Abbey on Location
should be addressed to:

Irregular Special Press
Endeavour House
170 Woodland Road
Sawston
Cambridge
CB22 3DX

❋❋❋❋❋ ⬤ ❋❋❋❋❋

1st edition 2013
2nd expanded edition 2017

Deluxe Full Colour Edition
ISBN: 978-1-901091-60-1 (13 digit)

Proof reading & editing: Roger Johnson
Front cover: Highclere Castle, the setting for *Downton Abbey*
Back cover: Matthew Crawley poses while filming at the Bluebell Railway

❋❋❋❋❋ ⬤ ❋❋❋❋❋

❋❋❋❋❋ ⬤ ❋❋❋❋❋

❋❋❋❋❋ ⬤ ❋❋❋❋❋

Contents

Contents

4

INTRODUCTION

'It's beautifully made – handsome, artfully crafted and acted. Smith, who plays the formidable and disdainful Dowager Countess, has a lovely way of delivering words, always spaced to perfection. This is going to be a treat if you like a lavish period drama of a Sunday evening.'

So wrote Sam Wollaston in *The Guardian* review of the first episode of *Downton Abbey*, which was aired on British television on the 26th September 2010. That episode had an audience of 9.2 million viewers, a 32% audience share, making *Downton Abbey* the most successful new drama series since *Whitechapel* in February 2009. The audience share has stayed around this level ever since.

Downton Abbey by film standards, though, is not a large production, so its success may be attributed to a number of elements. First is the writing by series creator Julian Fellowes, who had won an Oscar for Best Writing (Original Screenplay) for *Gosford Park* (2001). Although initially he was not keen to work on an Edwardian drama similar to *Gosford Park*, as envisaged by Gareth Neame of Carnival Films, he was soon persuaded and wrote the outline for the first series within a few weeks. Then there are the cleverly interlaced historical events, such as the sinking of the RMS Titanic, World War I, the Spanish influenza pandemic that followed it, and the Irish War of Independence. However, the best script in the world does not necessarily make for a hit show without the right actors to bring the whole thing to life. Here the casting director needs to be congratulated, for each actor involved is believable in their part, whether upstairs or downstairs, hero or villain. Beyond that, they have each become characters that the audience cares enough about to watch the next episode. For instance, when Brendan Coyle, who plays Bates, is put in prison, numerous fans wore 'Free Bates' T-shirts. Finally there are the locations, which are as much a character as any of the actors, and it is this element to which this book is devoted. It may interest the reader to learn just what preparation goes into location filming.

It all starts with a visit from the location manager, who surveys the possible location and discusses the requirements of the producer – and the price they are willing to pay. After successful negotiations comes the technical reconnaissance, several weeks before filming is due to take place. This visit involves all the production crew, director, set designer, lighting gaffer, camera crew and so forth. For example, when filming at the Bluebell

Railway[1] (page 188) the scenes to be filmed were worked out and notes taken of the sizes of signs, posters and so forth, so that the set dressing required to hide the non-period items could be made. Then just before filming there is the preparation day, which, as its name suggests, is when the props arrive and are placed in position. These vary in size from suitcases to horse drawn carriages to wooden brick walls. At the Bluebell Railway graphics were added to the station, to the locomotive to be used and to the carriages so as to represent the correct railway company (the Bluebell Railway belonged to Southern Railways, while the series is set in Yorkshire). Posters were put up, station name boards altered and any non-period items either removed or disguised. Lighting cables are also run out. Late in the evening and through the night

[A technical reconnaissance crew experiment with cut out lamp posts to ascertain where the best camera angles are to be had, and where to place additional prop lamp posts in advance of actual filming]

[1] The information on filming at the Bluebell Railway was kindly provided by Mick Blackburn, a long standing member of the railway, who has been involved with many such productions, large and small.

the unit base arrives from its previous location, which can be local or many hundreds of miles away. The unit base comprises the technical vehicles, production office, camera and lighting trucks, make-up and costume trucks, caravans for the artists – not forgetting the most important of all: the chuck wagon (the dining bus) as, just like an army, the production crew 'marches on its stomach'.

[Filming at the Bluebell Railway. Note that the Horsted Keynes station sign has been changed by the props department to Downton]

All must be set up and fully operational by 6.30 in the morning on the filming day. It is usually around this time that the extras will arrive to be dressed in their period costumes, while the actors are being made up. Camera positions are now finalised, with around four to five takes for each shot being acceptable. At a railway location this can become complicated, as the signalling does not allow for repeated arrivals and departures, so good communication between the film crew, locomotive crew and signalman is vital. Filming can also cause delays to any regular trains timetabled on that day, and of course once the public know about the filming they will generally want to watch, which means that they must be kept quietly out of shot. Once filming is complete, the cameras and lighting are the first to be packed away and moved onto the next location as soon as possible. Finally on the following day, the strike day, all the props and graphics are removed and the location reverts to normality until the next time.

And the result of all this effort, with around sixty-five people on set along with more than a hundred extras, is perhaps two minutes of usable footage. No wonder, then, that the series has received critical acclaim and won numerous accolades, including a Golden Globe and a Primetime Emmy, and is the most successful costume drama series since *Brideshead Revisited* in 1981.

I hope that you enjoy reading about all the wonderful places used in filming as much as I did researching them.

J. P. Sperati

DOWNTON ABBEY IN BERKSHIRE

ETON - ETON COLLEGE

[The Eton College playing fields behind Wall House were transformed into the site for the Thirsk fair. Note the group of boys to the right of the picture playing the Eton Wall Game.]

Eton, which until the local government reorganisation of 1974 was in Buckinghamshire, can be found on the opposite bank of the River Thames to Windsor. The High Street, running from Windsor Bridge right up to Eton College, is fortunate in having retained many of its characterful independent shops, although many of them now depend on the tourist trade. The High Street has also doubled as the fictional town of Causton in *Midsomer Murders*.

Eton College, founded by King Henry VI in 1440, is of course one of the most famous public schools in the country. The chapel, in the late Gothic or Perpendicular style, is less than half its intended length. Its completion was halted when Henry was deposed by Edward IV in 1461.

The splendid fan vaulting seen today was installed in the 1950s, after the wooden roof became infested with death watch beetle. It was completed in three years and is made of concrete, supported by steel trusses and faced with stone. The ribs that support each bay are hand-carved from Clipsham stone.

9

King Henry VI attached great importance to the religious aspects of his new foundation and he ensured that the fourteen daily services would be conducted on a magnificent scale by providing the chapel with no fewer than forty-six personnel, comprising priest fellows, chaplains, clerks and choristers. Today the chapel services still retain their key part in the life of the college: boys attend chapel once on Sundays in addition to compulsory services three or four days a week.

The wall paintings, which date from 1479-87 and are in the Flemish style, constitute the most remarkable work of art in the college. However, in 1560, as a result of an order from the new protestant church authorities, banning depiction of miracles, they were white-washed over and remained undiscovered until 1847. They were cleaned and restored in 1923.

One peculiar tradition of the College is the Eton Wall Game. It is not certain when it was first played but there are records that it was in existence in 1766. The rules have been revised over the years, although the game is essentially the same now as in 1849 when the rules were first put to paper. The field of play is a narrow strip of ground around five metres wide and 110 metres long, running beside an almost straight brick wall built in 1717. Each side tries to get its own ball down to the far end and score, but players may not handle the ball, or let any part of their bodies except feet and hands touch the ground, nor may they strike or hold an opponent. The final few metres at each end of the wall are called *calx* (Latin for chalk) and once here a player may lift up the ball against the wall with his foot and touch it with his hand. This earns a 'shy' worth one point, but more importantly allows the player to try for a goal, which is scored by throwing the ball at a door in a garden wall at one end, or a tree (originally a giant oak) at the other. This requires some skill, since the angle to the door is acute and the tree slim, but a successful player scores his team 10 points. For the spectators, mainly fellow pupils who look down on proceedings from a seated position on top of the wall, it is a dull game, but for the player it is far more fun than the rules suggest, and more exhausting and skilful as well.

The College has appeared countless times on both television and film, most notably in *The Jokers* (1967), *Henry VIII and His Six Wives* (1972), *Aces High* (1976), *Chariots of Fire* (1981), *The Secret Garden* (1993), *Young Sherlock Holmes* (1985), *The Fourth Protocol* (1987), *The Madness of King George* (1994), *Shakespeare in Love* (1998) and *Mansfield Park* (1999).

As far as *Downton Abbey* is concerned, the College featured in the 2012 Christmas Special, when the playing field behind Wall House was converted into a fair, full of food, games and modest dances. In the background of most shots the keen observer will be able to spot the wall, complete with chalk markings, as used for the Eton Wall Game. All the Downton staff (except for Carson) are eager to attend during the absence of the upstairs residents (apart from Branson, who drives everyone there).

[The arches under which Thomas becomes a hero]

It is here that the men of Downton win the tug-of-war, helped by the burly grocer, Jos Tufton, drafted into the team by Jimmy, who has astutely just placed a £1 bet on a Downton victory at the odds of ten to one. The subsequent winnings of £10 would have represented several weeks' wages, so it is no wonder he celebrated, and no wonder he attracted the attention of muggers. He was fortunate to have Thomas on hand to step in and take the beating for him. This scene was filmed under one of the arches carrying the B3022 (Slough Road) over Colenorton Brook which feeds Fellow's Pond.

Finally in Baldwin's Shore, just off High Street, will be found a red-bricked building with an archway. This opening was fitted out with windows and set dressed to become Tufton's shop front. This allowed for the camera to be positioned inside the 'shop' and to look out through the window to where Thomas, accompanied by Jimmy and Alfred, admire the range of spices on sale in the window.

LOWER BASILDON - BASILDON PARK

[The Palladian front at Basildon Park]

The village of Lower Basildon, close to Pangbourne, is the site of a small Roman villa that was discovered in 1839 during the construction of the Great Western Railway. Despite its size it did have two superb mosaic floors, which were unfortunately destroyed almost immediately. The agriculturist Jethro Tull was born in the parish and was also buried here in the churchyard of St. Bartholomew's. Just outside the village on the Streatley road is the Basildon Grotto consisting of a rock chamber filled with shells dating from 1720. Today Grotto House is the headquarters of the Institute for Sport, Parks and Leisure.

The area is best known though for the National Trust Grade I listed property Basildon Park. The house was built for Sir Francis Sykes between 1776 and 1783 in the Palladian style, although the interior is in the neoclassical style, which was becoming more fashionable at the time. In fact the house was never completed due to the reduced circumstances of Sir Francis who lost much of his money as a result of the crash of the East India Company. On his death the house passed to his son who died a few weeks later. In turn it passed to his grandson who was only 5-years-old. It was he who became immortalised by Charles Dickens in *Oliver Twist* as the cruel and villainous character Bill Sikes – this coming about when his wife Lady Sykes was found to be having an affair with the painter Daniel

Maclise resulting in Sir Francis publically denouncing Maclise, who just happened to be a close friend of Dickens.

Soon afterwards the estate was sold to James Morrison who brought a period of stability. Just like Downton Abbey the house, still owned by the Morrison family, was used as a convalescent hospital during World War I. Afterwards there was a succession of owners until 1929 when it was stripped of many of its fixtures and fittings and all but abandoned. During World War II it was again requisitioned, but this time became a barracks and training ground for tanks, and, latterly, a prisoner of war camp. Following the war the house was left to fall into ruin. However, salvation was at hand for the second Lord Iliffe, who lived in the area, was persuaded by his wife to buy the property. Over the next quarter of a century a complete restoration and refurnishing took place. Finally in 1978 the Iliffes gave the estate to the National Trust.

The house can be seen in such productions as *Pride and Prejudice* (2005), *Marie-Antoinette* (2006), *Dorian Gray* (2009) and *Pride and Prejudice and Zombies* (2016).

As far as *Downton Abbey* is concerned Basildon Park provides the interior setting for the Crawley's London home, Grantham House (page 86). In addition the picnic scene that was supposed to take place in Hyde Park was largely filmed in the grounds (page 116).

The main rooms used include the staircase hall located at the centre of the house. This is a double height room lit by a clerestory with a cantilever staircase, which rises in flights around three of the four walls to the gallery on the first floor. The balustrade is gilded wrought iron adorned with medallions featuring classical motifs.

The Octagon Room on the first floor is the principal room of the house and became the drawing room where Rose and Atticus's engagement party is held at the end of the fifth series. It has an ornate gilded ceiling with recessed panels in the Italian Renaissance style, installed in 1840. As is to be expected from its name it is an eight-sided room with windows on three of the walls to the front forming a large bay. The walls themselves are hung with red felt making it instantly recognisable whenever it makes an appearance on television.

Adjacent to the Octagon Room is the dining room, not ideally placed since the kitchens are on the ground floor and some distance away in the North Pavilion (not part of the main house), no doubt resulting in many a cold meal being served. The dining room decoration was inspired by Robert

Adam with the ceiling being originally divided into panels, as were the walls, and decorated with either mirrors or paintings depicting classical scenes. However, these were sold in 1929 and can now be seen in the Basildon Room of the Waldorf Astoria Hotel in New York. The bare room was later redecorated by Lord and Lady Iliffe who had the room painted and turned into a drawing room. The room has since been redeveloped by artist Alec Cobbe in style similar to the original scheme so is once again neoclassical. The room became the ballroom for the coming-out ball at which the Prince of Wales asks Rose for the first dance at the conclusion of *Downton Abbey* series four (*The London Season*).

DOWNTON ABBEY IN BUCKINGHAMSHIRE

BEACONSFIELD - HALL BARN, HALL PLACE

The name Beaconsfield is actually a corruption of Bekensfield, meaning a 'clearing in the Beeches'. Being conveniently situated close to the M40 motorway and having a mainline railway service to London as well, the area has become a sought-after place to live, and with so many fascinating buildings and history is also a great favourite with film crews. Like nearby Amersham it is split up into two parts, the Old Town and the New Town.

Walking through the Old Town feels like stepping back in time. With so many listed buildings, it is almost completely unspoilt. Its situation midway between London and Oxford made the Old Town an ideal stopping place *en-route* for horse-drawn coaches. There are still many signs of these enchanting old coaching inns and hostelries to be found today. Interestingly, it consists of four sections of road known as 'ends' – Aylesbury End, London End, Windsor End and Wycombe End – it is where the coach routes from these destinations met.

Benjamin Disraeli was the First Earl of Beaconsfield, and one of the town's famous residents was the children's novelist Enid Blyton. She lived at a house named Green Hedges from 1938 until her death in 1968. Unfortunately the house has been demolished to make way for newer properties. However, you are able to see a detailed miniature version at the Bekonscot model village. Reputed to be the oldest model village in the world, it is situated in the heart of the New Town.

Beaconsfield manor, originally part of the manor of Burnham, was subdivided in three estates: Hall Barn, Gregories and Whiltones, now known as Wilton Park. In 1624, Anne Waller and her son, Edmund acquired the lands of Hall Barn. Later Edmund became a well-known poet and politician. He was arrested in 1643 for his part in a plot to establish London as a stronghold for King Charles I and sentenced to death, but managed to avoid this through a lavish bribe (paying a £10,000 fine) and by betraying his fellow conspirators (Richard Challoner and Nathaniel Tomkins) who were both executed. Waller's only punishment was to be banished from the realm. During his banishment he travelled through France, Switzerland and Italy returning to Beaconsfield in 1655, and it is thought that it was at this time that he designed and built the house of Hall Barn. He was now a more careful man writing poetic tributes to both Oliver Cromwell in 1655, and King Charles II in 1660. In fact he was called upon by the King to explain why his eulogy to Cromwell was seen as superior to

15

that on himself. Rather tactfully Waller is said to have replied, "Sir, we poets never succeed so well in writing truth as in fiction".

[The home of Sir Anthony Strallan is in fact Hall Barn in Beaconsfield]

After the death of his second wife, Mary Bracey, in 1677 he retired to Hall Barn, dying there in 1687. He was buried at the local church of St. Mary and All Saints. Hall Barn remained in the family for several generations, being occupied from 1687 to 1708 by Waller's son, Edmund Waller II. The younger Edmund's widow married John Aislabie, who created Studley Royal in North Yorkshire, and from around 1713 some significant landscaping was undertaken, including the erection of various garden buildings and ornaments.

In 1832 the estate was sold to Sir Gore Ousley, who developed it further until his death in 1844. From 1880 the then-owner Edward Levy-Lawson, 1st Lord Burnham, enlarged the house and reworked the gardens. The 20th century brought two disasters, one man-made, the other natural, which altered the landscape forever. In the 1970s the new M40 motorway was built in a cutting across the northern part of the estate, separating the main entrance from the house (which is connected by a bridge across the motorway). The second disaster was the storms of 1987 and 1990 which brought down many of the mature woodland trees, particularly in The Grove.

In *Downton Abbey* Hall Barn became the residence of Sir Anthony Strallan, the local landowner and widower, who so nearly married Lady Edith, only abandoning her at the altar. Some internal filming was done at the house although the production company brought in their own furniture for these scenes.

The house is not open to the public, but the gardens (some 200 hectares) are part of the National Gardens Scheme and can be visited at certain times of the year (see www.ngs.org.uk for further information). In addition the Chiltern Shakespeare Company have mounted productions in the gardens, for which a covered raked seating auditorium is constructed each time (see www.chiltern-shakespeare.co.uk).

At Wycombe End, just by the main crossroads in Beaconsfield Old Town, is Hall Place, formerly known as The Rectory, and now a Grade II listed building.

The house dates from the middle of the 18th century when it was owned by one H. Woodyer. It was redesigned in the late 19th century, and restored in the 1990s to this design by the current owners, Dr. and Mrs. Gary Bell. The house is built of red brick and comprises two storeys and an attic with dormer windows.

The gardens date from as early as the 16th century, with some portions of the garden wall containing triangular and four sided recesses, thought to be bee boles. Unfortunately the garden is not as extensive as it once was, having been built on, and the land now belonging to several different parties. If you intend to visit, please note that Hall Place is a private property and not open to the public

[The interior scenes at Isobel Crawley's house were filmed a Hall Place in the centre of the Old Town]

Manorial documents survive from the 14th and 15th century referring to Hallelond (Hall Barn) Manor. This is not Edmund Waller's Hall Barn, which had yet to be built, but a property that in 1385 was under the ownership of Hugh Berwick, who was also, it transpires, a tenant at Beaconsfield Manor. Hall Barn Manor no longer survives but it is thought to have been located on, or near, the site of the old rectory at Hall Place. By the middle of the 19th century Hall Place was used as a private boarding school.

It is the interior of Hall Place which is of most interest to *Downton Abbey* fans, since the ground floor rooms, which feature some fine 17th century wood panelling (including a mid-17th century wooden fireplace), were used for the Downton home of Isobel Crawley. The exterior shots, however, were all done at Bampton (page 149). At first glance the house looks similar to that of the Dowager Countess but should not be confused with that property, which is Byfleet Manor in Surrey (page 175).

CHALFONT ST. GILES - CHILTERN OPEN AIR MUSEUM

[Lady Edith cycles past this part of the Chiltern Open Air Museum on her way to John Drake's farm]

In the Domesday Book Chalfont St. Giles and neighbouring Chalfont St. Peter are listed as separate manors with different owners. During the Great Plague of London in 1665, John Milton retired to the village, where he completed *Paradise Lost*. The whole area is said to be exclusive, and due to its many celebrity residents it has been referred to as a 'mini Hollywood'. Along with neighbouring Gerrards Cross this is the most expensive postcode in which to buy property outside of central London.

Chiltern Open Air Museum is home to thirty-three historic buildings rescued from destruction around the Chiltern Hills and surrounding areas, and re-erected in 45 acres of beautiful traditional Chilterns landscapes. The historic building collections, which span 2000 years of the region's history, include a reconstructed iron age house, a Victorian working farm, a tin chapel, cottages, and rural industries such as a working blacksmith's forge and a furniture factory.

There are yet more historic buildings in storage, including the Jackson Recording Studios from Maple Cross, several medieval town buildings, an Abbey Barn, and Victorian industrial buildings such as pig sties from Princes Risborough, a Saddlery from Aylesbury and a traditional

19

commercial bake oven from Chesham. As the Museum is a charity, all funds for capital projects have to be sourced to enable the structure to be re-erected and displayed.

Visitors can explore the range of dwellings and workplaces, many of them furnished, such as the 1947 prefab from Amersham or the Victorian Toll House from High Wycombe. Museum volunteers help tell the story of these buildings, and visitors can dress up in period clothing, play with replica and real traditional toys, and try their hand at constructing model buildings. An exciting programme of special events each year also helps to highlight aspects of life that these buildings have seen over the centuries. Young visitors are encouraged to get involved during the holidays with family activities and to join the holiday clubs in the school vacations.

The Museum not only conserves these wonderful vernacular buildings, structures that would otherwise have been destroyed, but also preserves the traditional skills used in the construction and repair of historic buildings and agricultural life generally. Past projects have included reconstructing medieval thatching techniques on a cruck barn from Arborfield and the reconstruction of a rescued earth cottage made from wytchert – white clay found only in the Vale of Aylesbury and mixed with straw.

The historic Chilterns farmstead is a popular feature, with its working farm machinery and livestock. Staff and volunteers are gradually developing the special local character of the farm, a process that involves the creation of roughly thatched hovels to protect equipment, the development of a rick yard with a corn rick and stock yard. The farm buildings include a cart shed from Gorhambury, a cattle byre from Borehamwood, a granary from Rossway, and a stable, cattle byre and cart shed from Marsworth farm. The Museum's historic farm equipment being restored to use includes a thrashing machine, a reaper binder, a seed drill and several local carts and wagons. Traditional crops are grown at the museum, cultivated and harvested using traditional techniques, including stooking the corn (bundles or sheaves of corn stood upright in groups to dry out before being placed in a corn rick).

The working farm includes traditional animal breeds including Oxford Down Sheep, Dorking Silver Grey Chickens and heavy horses. In April visitors may see lambing taking place in the reconstructed Chilterns Lambing Fold, with its roughly thatched shelters and a shepherd's living van. Animal feed is often supplemented with home grown hay, which is stored in traditional hay ricks, thatched to keep the hay dry until winter when it is needed for the animals.

The landscape is well worth seeing too. The historic buildings are surrounded by Chilterns parkland and downland, and there is a lovely woodland walk, with bluebells in the spring. Dogs are welcome on a short leash, so the Museum provides a great backdrop for walks in most seasons.

[The tree trunk prior to the attentions of Lady Edith]

The Museum is a popular television location, having featured in episodes of *Midsomer Murders* and *Call the Midwife*, and in every series of *Horrible Histories*. It may also be spotted in comedy programmes, such as *Harry and Paul* and *Mitchell and Webb*.

As far as *Downton Abbey* is concerned, four scenes were shot here. This is the farm where Lady Edith helps out in episode 2.2. She has discovered that farmer John Drake is in need, being unable to drive himself, and having lost to the war effort his only farmhand who can drive, so she promptly volunteers to drive Drake's tractor. Following her arrival at the farm by bicycle, she is next seen on a tractor helping uproot a tree trunk, which after some initial grinding of gears she performs rather expertly, to the obvious delight of the farmer.

Mrs. Drake, accompanied by a sheepdog, then arrives with a basket of food, which they eat in the barn, where the canine takes a fancy to the comestibles, prompting some unscripted remarks from the actors.

21

[The cart used in filming is one of the Museum exhibits (top).
The barn where Drake and Edith eat and later kiss (bottom)]

Later in the same episode we see Edith and Drake loading hay onto a cart. They decide to take a break, and Drake offers Edith something alcoholic from a bottle, at which point Drake's wife again appears, but this time she is not so friendly, as she now suspects her husband of harbouring feelings for Lady Edith. The final scene takes place inside the barn at night, when Edith succumbs to the farmer's advances, and they kiss, not knowing that Mrs. Drake is watching from the other side of the yard. The next we learn of this budding romance is at breakfast (presumably the following morning) when the Earl of Grantham receives a letter from Mrs. Drake informing him that Edith's services will no longer be required as they are going to take on a new farmhand.

A visit to this beautiful site in the Chiltern Hills is a magical experience, offering a fantastic day out for all the family. The Museum is usually open seven days a week from the beginning of April to the end of October, but visitors should check each season's dates on the website (www.coam.org.uk) beforehand. Schools and pre-booked groups are welcome from February to November.

HALTON - HALTON HOUSE

Halton is a small village in the Vale of Aylesbury, about two miles from Wendover and five from Aylesbury itself. The Wendover arm of the Grand Union Canal flows through the village on its course from Wendover to Marsworth lock, near Tring.

The area is dominated by R.A.F. Halton, a training station with a grass airfield used for glider training. The base had a large military hospital employing thousands of people, which was closed in 1995. The buildings have since been demolished in favour of the Princess Mary Gate housing scheme.

In 1913 Alfred de Rothschild, who owned the Halton Estate, invited no. 3 Squadron of the Royal Flying Corps to use his land for summer manoeuvres, the first flight being recorded on the 18th September. At the outbreak of World War I Rothschild offered Lord Kitchener the use of the estate for the British Army, and by 1916 the area was covered in tents, with some twenty thousand troops under training. That same year the R.F.C. moved its air mechanics school from Farnborough to Halton, and in 1917 the school was permanently housed there in workshops constructed by German prisoners of war.

[Halton House doubles as the interior of Haxby Hall]

Alfred de Rothschild died in January 1918, and the War Office seized the opportunity to purchase the whole estate on behalf of the Royal Air Force, which would come into being in April of that year. The price paid was £112,000; clearly a bargain, for included in the sale was the family residence, Halton House (one of several houses owned by the Rothschilds), built in 1883 in a French style.

It had been the scene for Alfred's sparkling weekend house parties, which attracted the cream of British society. Today it is the Officers' Mess. In fact there had been a house on the site since the Norman Conquest, at which time it belonged to the Archbishop of Canterbury. In the mid-16th century Thomas Cranmer sold it to Henry Bradshaw, the Chancellor of the Exchequer. In 1720 it was in turn sold to Sir Francis Dashwood and in 1853 became the property of Lionel de Rothschild. However, the house became uninhabited and was in ruins when the estate, comprising some one-and-a-half thousand acres, was given to Alfred de Rothschild who demolished the house. The new building that sprang up in just three years is very much influenced by nearby Waddesdon Manor (page 27), the home of Baron Ferdinand de Rothschild, his brother-in-law. Although not as large it does have many of the same architectural features, such as classical pediments jutting out from mansard roofs, spires, gables and a giant cupola. In fact it was described as looking somewhat like a giant wedding cake.

The inside was furnished in what is known as *le style Rothschild*, i.e. 18th century French furniture, boulle, ebony, and ormolu, complemented by Old Masters and fine porcelain.

In 1919, Lord Trenchard established the No. 1 School of Technical Training at R.A.F. Halton, where it remained until 1993 when it was moved to R.A.F. Cosford. In addition, during World War II the base was host to 112 and 402 Squadrons of the Royal Canadian Air Force.

Today the establishment is the gateway to the Royal Air Force and, although it no longer trains aircraft engineers, it does provide nine weeks of basic training before recruits continue on their individual trade training. In October 1997, R.A.F. Halton was honoured with a Queen's Colour in recognition of its outstanding contribution to training over many years. The Trenchard Museum, which is dedicated to the history of the base, is open to the public on Tuesdays.

[The main atrium where Sir Richard and Lady Mary discuss whether to purchase the house for their marital home]

Halton House has featured in a number of television and film productions including *Jeeves and Wooster*, *Evita* (1996), *An Ideal Husband* (1999), *The World Is Not Enough* (1999), *What a Girl Wants* (2003), *The Queen* (2006), *Flyboys* (2006) and *The King's Speech* (2010). It appeared briefly in episode 2.6 of *Downton Abbey* as the house which Sir Richard Carlisle takes Lady Mary to view as their prospective marital home. From positions on opposite sides on the galleried landing, the two discuss whether they should save this now abandoned property and "give the house another chapter" as Sir Richard puts it. Lady Mary quips that "I suppose one has to live somewhere".

Fact is rather stranger than fiction, since at the time this episode is set the estate in real life would have been a hive of activity and swarming with military personnel, while the house itself, as mentioned, may well have been empty following the death of Alfred de Rothschild, pending its eventual sale to the War Office.

The Rothschild connection is subtly emphasised by the establishing exterior shot of Haxby Hall, which does not show Halton House, but the larger Waddesdon Manor (page 27), the seat of Alfred de Rothschild's brother-in-law, Baron Ferdinand de Rothschild. And for further proof, one need look no further than the gallery where Sir Richard and Lady Mary converse. In the ironwork, and clearly in shot, is the enduring symbol of the Rothschild family, five arrows, which was first granted in an Austrian patent for arms in 1817 (with the grant from the College of Arms in London for the same design being successfully petitioned the following year).

HEDSOR - HEDSOR HOUSE

In the very south of the county, close to Bourne End is the village of Hedsor, which in Old English means Haedde's cliff, referring to the fact that the village is situated on a cliff overlooking the River Thames.

Hedsor House was the ancient family seat of the de Hedsors who are first mentioned in the Domesday book of 1086. In the 18th century it was a royal residence for Princess Augusta, Dowager Princess of Wales with royalty being frequent visitors to the estate from nearby Windsor Castle. The house was originally designed by Sir William Chambers, architect of Somerset House in London. However, the building was badly damaged by fire in 1795 with the rebuild not being completed until 1868. It was now in the style of an Italian villa and featured a domed hall, which rightly became the focal point of the house. The estate has grounds extending to 85-acres and here may be found the Hedsor Folly built by Baron Boston to commemorate the famous victory at Waterloo in 1815.

Today the house is described as a 'Georgianised' version of a Victorian house. It is in private hands and operated as a location for corporate events and weddings. It is not open to the public.

[Hedsor House makes an ideal venue for a fashion show]

On film it may be spotted in *The Golden Compass* (2007), *Brighton Rock* (2010), *Quartet* (2012), *Red 2* (2015), *Mortdecai* (2015) and *Legend* (2015) as well as in series such as *Midsomer Murders* and *Mr. Selfridge*. As far as *Downton Abbey* is concerned the house was used to very good effect as the location for the fashion show in episode 4.5. It is here Lady Mary – accompanied by Lady Rosamund – meets Mabel Lane Fox – accompanied by Charles Blake – for the first time and concludes that she is "… not at all what I imagined".

WADDESDON - WADDESDON MANOR

To call Waddesdon Manor a country house is somewhat of an understatement – it is actually a neo-renaissance building in the style of a French chateau, as found in the Loire Valley, with a large estate around it. Ornate luxury comes to mind when looking at the magnificent large mansion, not a surprise considering that it was built for Baron Ferdinand de Rothschild. His chosen architect was Gabriel-Hippolyte Destailleur.

It may look old-fashioned on the outside, but on the inside, the Baron had the most modern innovations of the 19th century incorporated, such as a steel frame, which permits the layout of the upper floors to be totally different from that of the lower floors. It also has hot and cold running water in its bathrooms, central heating and an electric bell system as well as electric lighting. The Manor housed an extensive French 18th century collection of fine art as well as English and Dutch paintings, some of which were passed on to the British Museum as the 'Waddesdon Bequest' after the Baron died in 1898.

[Waddesdon Manor in bloom]

The gardens were landscaped extensively, under the guidance of the French landscape architect Lainé. Not a mean feat as the hilltop was barren, and several fully-grown trees were planted, some so big it took sixteen horses to move them to their new location. It is regarded as one of the finest Victorian gardens in Britain. Queen Victoria invited herself to view the park, but is reported to have been more fascinated by the new invention of electric lighting that had been installed – it is said that she spent ten minutes switching a chandelier on and off. While some collections were bequeathed, following generations of Rothschilds have added to the fine art and furniture collections, and they continue to be a draw for visitors.

The grounds and property have been owned by the National Trust (www.waddesdon.org.uk) since 1957, but continue to be administered by a

Rothschild family trust as a semi-independent operation, which is an unprecedented arrangement – normally the National Trust does that itself once it takes ownership of a property, and former owners tend to be no longer involved. James de Rothschild bequeathed the Manor and its contents along with two hundred acres of grounds and the largest ever endowment to the National Trust – £750,000. Eythrope and the rest of the Waddesdon estate remain in the Rothschild family's possession. The Rothschilds tended to reside around the borders of Hertfordshire and Buckinghamshire, an area unofficially known as 'Rothschildshire', and at one point they owned seven large country houses and thirty thousand acres of land in the area, and further afield another forty great Rothschild properties across Europe. The current baron, Jacob Rothschild, 4th Lord Rothschild, has overseen a major restoration and introduced new collections.

On 10th June 2003, approximately one hundred, irreplaceable and priceless, French gold snuff boxes and bejewelled trifles were stolen, none of which has thus far been recovered. There is still a reward on offer for information leading to their recovery.

Films that made use of the stunning house and gardens include *Carry On Don't Lose Your Head* (1966), *Never Say Never Again* (1983), *An Ideal Husband* (1999), *Daniel Deronda* (2002), *The Tenth Kingdom* (2000) and *The Queen* (2006) starring Dame Helen Mirren, where it stood in for Buckingham Palace gardens. Its appearance in *Downton Abbey* is fleeting, as it appears only in an establishing shot of Haxby Hall, which Sir Richard Carlisle takes Lady Mary to view when they are looking for suitable properties to purchase as their marital home. The interior scenes, however, were all done at nearby Halton House (page 23).

WEST WYCOMBE - WEST WYCOMBE PARK

West Wycombe Park, conceived as a pleasure palace for the 18th century libertine and dilettante Sir Francis Dashwood, was built between 1740 and 1800, near the village of West Wycombe in Buckinghamshire. The house, designed as a long rectangle with four columned and pedimented facades, may be said to encapsulate the entire progression of British 18th century architecture, from early idiosyncratic Palladian to the Neoclassical. The finest architects of the day were invited to submitted plans for transforming the older family house into a modern architectural extravaganza. The great Robert Adam offered a plan for the west portico, but his idea was never adopted.

The mansion is set within landscaped grounds, containing many small temples and follies which act as satellites to the house itself. The park is unique in its consistent use of classical architecture from both Greece and Italy. The two principal architects of the gardens were John Donowell and Nicholas Revett, who designed all of the ornamental buildings in the park. The landscape architect Thomas Cook began to execute the plans for the estate, with a nine-acre man-made lake created in the form of a swan from the nearby River Wye. The lake originally had a Spanish galleon for the amusement of Dashwood's guests, complete with a resident captain on board.

[Main entrance to West Wycombe Park, home of the Dashwoods]

The Temple of Apollo, originally constructed as a gateway, was later used for cock fighting; it also screened the view of the domestic service wing from the main house. The Temple of the Winds, a curious octagonal tower, was design in imitation of the Tower of the Winds in Athens. The Temple of Music, on an island in the lake, was inspired by the Temple of Vesta in

Rome. Opposite the temple and flanked by reclining statues of water nymphs, is the garden's main cascade. The cascade that we see today is a replica of the original, which was demolished in the 1830s.

The classical theme continues along the path around the lake, with the Temple of Daphne and a hidden summerhouse called the Temple of Flora, both reminiscent of a small temple on the Acropolis. Also hidden away is the Round Temple with its curved loggia. A small niche at the Temple of Diana contains a statue of the goddess. Below the Temple of Venus is the Exedra, a high flint wall with an alcove in which stands a statue of Mercury, and a grotto known as Venus's Parlour. The temple once held a copy of the Venus de' Medici; it was demolished in the 1820s but has recently been reconstructed and now holds a replica of the Venus de Milo.

Although the house is now owned by the National Trust, it remains the home of Sir Edward Dashwood and his family. It is open to the public during the summer months.

This most picturesque of locations may be spotted in a number of film productions, the most notable of which include *Another Country* (1984), *Dead Man's Folly* (1986), *An Ideal Husband* (1999), *The Importance of Being Earnest* (2002), *What a Girl Wants* (2003) and *The Duchess* (2008). On the small screen it has appeared in *Foyle's War*, *Lewis*, *Cranford*, and *Marple: A Pocket Full of Rye*.

The interior doubles for Downton Abbey, most notably in episode 1.6, as the Dowager Countess and Lady Cora discuss whether Lady Mary will accept Matthew. Cora's uncertainty prompts the Dowager to reply "Well, if she doesn't, we'll just have to take her abroad. In these moments, you can normally find an Italian who isn't too picky". It also appears as the interior of Robert's sister, Lady Rosamund Painswick, London house (page 95), which she seems happy to share with her brother and his family, whenever they are in London and need accommodation. Rather curiously in episode 6.9 the grounds double for those at Downton Abbey as the family walk and talk at very start of the episode, with shots being skilfully mixed between the two sites to make it look like just one location.

DOWNTON ABBEY IN COUNTY DURHAM

BEAMISH - BEAMISH MUSEUM

Pit Hill, around 10 miles north-west of Durham, was the original name given to the village of Beamish, which is contained within Hell Hole Wood. The area is best known for the Beamish Museum (officially the North of England Open Air Museum), which opened in 1972. It is set in 300 acres of beautiful County Durham countryside, and vividly illustrates life in North East England in the 1820s, 1910s and 1940s.

Beamish is unique. Perhaps it's the friendly costumed characters – tram drivers, shop keepers, enginemen and pitmen's wives. Or maybe it's the pit cottages, old shops, village school, farm and town street. Whatever it is, more than 750,000 visitors from throughout the U.K. and overseas take a trip back in time each year at this award-winning museum.

[Beamish Museum showing the Motor & Cycle Works, which were to become those of 'Talbot and Branson']

Visitors stroll down the cobbled street of The Town, to see the dentist's home and surgery, solicitor's office and period branch of Barclay & Co's Bank. There is a splendid Masonic hall to explore, along with fully stocked Co-operative shops, a newspaper office, carriage house and livery stables. The early days of motoring are on view in the Motor & Cycle Works and delicious boiled sweets are made and sold in the Jubilee Confectionery. Tasty bread, cakes and biscuits are made at Herron's Bakery, using traditional recipes and equipment and there's the chance to sample the

33

goods and buy a treat to take home. In May 2016, the newest attractions opened in The Town – an early 1900s chemist's shop, with dispensary and aerated waters plant, and photographers' studio, where visitors can have their picture taken in period costume.

Nearby is The Pit Village with a row of miner's cottages, a Methodist chapel and village school, a silver band practise hall and a real, coal-fired fish & chip shop where visitors can enjoy a delicious taste of the past.

An underground tour at the drift mine begins with a tour of the colliery lamp cabin and in the heapstead, a magnificent steam winding engine demonstrates how men, ponies and coal were brought to the surface. Nearby are the newly-opened pit pony stables housing some of the museum's seven Shetland pit ponies.

Pockerley Old Hall is based on a mediaeval fortified manor house and recreates rural life of almost two hundred years ago. The small manor house, its terraced gardens and costume of the day are in complete contrast to the lifestyle of the early 1900s which the other attractions at Beamish portray.

The 1825 steam railway at Pockerley Waggonway illustrates the days of railway pioneering. A working replica of an early 1800s 'lost locomotive', *The Steam Elephant*, has been researched and built using contemporary illustrations for guidance. *The Steam Elephant* works, alongside a replica of Stephenson's *Locomotion No. 1* and Hedley's *Puffing Billy*, taking visitors on a short ride in recreated carriages from the early days of rail travel.

The 1940s Farm is set in the period from 1942 to 1944, a snapshot of life on the Home Front during World War II. North Eastern farmers played a huge part in helping Britain to win the war with intensive farming saving the nation from starvation. The 1940s Farm tells the everyday story of the family who live there and the people brought in to supplement the workforce with tales of Land Girls, evacuees and the Home Guard.

It is should be no surprise to learn that Beamish is popular with television producers, and has made over 300 appearances over the years including *Dark Angel*, *Fifteen Streets*, *The Black Candle*, *The Wingless Bird*, *The Monocled Mutineer* and *Joe Maddison's War*. For *Downton Abbey* viewers had to wait until the very final episode of series 6 to see Lady Mary, Tom Branson and Henry Talbot emerge from the passageway next to the sweet shop to look across the road towards the Motor & Cycle Works.

[*Downton Abbey* filming in the fake snow in July 2015]

Lady Mary professes to hate surprises and then asks, "Well, what am I looking at?" The obvious does not dawn on her for a moment, until she notices that the sign on the Beamish Motor & Cycle Works reads Talbot & Branson Motors. "But it looks like a going concern," she exclaims. As she is given a tour she soon discovers that it is a proper business, as well as being the perfect solution for both the ex-chauffeur and ex-racing driver who are now in partnership. Lady Mary points out, "All of which means you're second-hand car salesmen," but far from being disappointed it makes her "as proud as anybody living" at which point she whispers to Henry that she is pregnant.

A full programme of special events takes place at Beamish throughout the year. From the Great North Festival of Transport to a Georgian Fair and the Festival of Fifties, there's something for all the family to enjoy. To find out the opening times, prices and information on special events see the Beamish Museum web pages (www.beamish.org.uk).

DOWNTON ABBEY IN HAMPSHIRE

HIGHCLERE & BURGHCLERE - HIGHCLERE CASTLE PORTAL HALL

As magnificent as its fictional counterpart, Highclere Castle is the home, not of Lord and Lady Grantham but of Lord and Lady Carnarvon. Despite the fact that for at least a century its postal address has been 'Highclere Castle, Newbury, Berkshire', the 'real' Downton Abbey is actually in Hampshire! The mail for the village of Highclere is naturally delivered from the nearest town, which in this case happens to be just over the border, in the neighbouring county.

[A view of Highclere Castle that will be instantly recognisable to any *Downton Abbey* fan]

The house, built in the Jacobean style, is situated about 5 miles south of Newbury, in 1,000 acres of spectacular parkland, landscaped by Lancelot 'Capability' Brown. The estate has been the home of the Herbert family since 1679, the Earldom of Carnarvon being created by King George III in

1793. Today Highclere is the home of the 8th Earl, George Reginald Oliver Molyneux Herbert, and his family, who live in the castle during the winter, and in a cottage in the grounds during the summer, when the house is open to visitors. They are closely involved with the estate and its running.

Lord and Lady Carnarvon see themselves as stewards of the house and the estate, looking after it for future generations. This feeling of *noblesse oblige* is similar to that expressed by the Earl of Grantham about his role in life in the television series – Downton Abbey is his life's work.

The family also vacate the castle when weddings are held there, but they move back in when filming takes place. Lady Carnarvon says she wouldn't expect any of her staff to be there at 7 am to let the television crew in.

An Iron Age fort (Beacon Hill) and an early Anglo-Saxon charter show that the area has been inhabited for some 1,300 years, although the records are sketchy until the Georgian era.

Highclere Castle was originally built to a square classical design, but the 3rd Earl of Carnarvon commissioned Sir Charles Barry, fresh from finishing the Palace of Westminster in London, to remodel the house between 1839 and 1842 into the building standing here today. Underneath are the foundations of the medieval palace of the Bishops of Winchester, owners of the estate from the 8th century onwards, and registered as such in the Domesday Book. The present house is an imposing Grade I listed mansion.

The interior was completed in 1878, eighteen years after Barry's death, by his assistant Thomas Allom. The castle became a political centre, one of the first visitors being Benjamin Disraeli, who exclaimed, "How scenical! How scenical!" on seeing the building. The guest books record house parties full of politicians, technological innovators, aviators, soldiers and Egyptologists.

At the outbreak of World War I, Almina, the 5th Countess of Carnarvon, turned the castle into a hospital for soldiers, and worked as a nurse herself – a story similar to one of the plots in *Downton Abbey*. Julian Fellowes is actually a longstanding friend of the Carnarvons, and had Highclere Castle already in mind when first called upon to write the scripts.

Countess Almina was the beloved illegitimate daughter of Alfred de Rothschild, who built Halton House in Buckinghamshire (page 23). When the war ended, Highclere became a private home again, until World War II, when it briefly offered a home for evacuee children from north London.

The 5th Earl of Carnarvon, Almina's husband, first visited Egypt in 1898, and from 1906 was a dedicated amateur archaeologist and collector of antiquities. The Egyptian Exhibition in the castle's cellar contains artefacts from the explorations he undertook with Howard Carter before 1922. In November that year, the two men opened the famous tomb of the Egyptian boy pharaoh Tutankhamen. Sadly, the following March the Earl suffered a mosquito bite which became infected, and although Countess Almina flew to Egypt with a surgeon, he died shortly after. It is reported that at the same moment, back at Highclere his beloved fox terrier howled once, and dropped dead. Lord Carnarvon's death was partly responsible for the legend of a curse on the tomb. The man and his canine companion are buried together on Beacon Hill, near the village of Burghclere (page 46), about a mile from the castle. Beacon Hill is open to the public.

The death duties owing were severe, and although many tradesmen refused to take payment for their services, remembering Lady Carnarvon's kindness and help during the war, she was obliged to sell much of the Egyptian collection. Most of the items were purchased by the Metropolitan Museum of New York, but Howard Carter commented that a "few unimportant" artefacts had been left at Highclere, tucked away in hidden cupboards. They were only re-discovered by the Carnarvon family in 1987, and an exhibition was set up in the Antiquities Room. These items include jewellery, figures, and, most excitingly, the coffin of a noblewoman from 3,500 years ago.

[The main entrance (left), saloon (right)]

Of course, visiting *Downton Abbey* fans will recognise many parts of the house, like the main entrance, set in honey-coloured Bath stone, and the gravel driveway leading up to it, on which Carson lines up the staff to greet such important visitors as the Duke of Crowborough.

The exact number of rooms in the castle is uncertain, figures given ranging from 200 to 300, but the heart of the house, physically and socially, is certainly the saloon on the ground floor, designed in a gothic style for the 4th Earl by Thomas Allom. The wall coverings of hand-tooled leather, dating from 1631, were brought by the 3rd Earl from Cordoba in Spain, and were hung up here in 1862. The Rijksmuseum in Amsterdam has matching panels on display.

[The State Dining Room (left) and library (right)]

Dominating the State Dining Room is the great portrait of King Charles I on horseback, by Sir Anthony van Dyck, the famous Flemish artist who became the English King's favoured painter. On either side are portraits of Carnarvon ancestors dating from the 1640s. Another version of van Dyck's painting is in the royal collection, and more of his portraits of King Charles can be seen at the National Gallery in London (page 74) and at the Louvre in Paris. The artist died in London in 1641, and was buried at St. Paul's Cathedral, where the King erected a monument in his memory.

Highclere Castle also houses a double library with over 5,650 books, some dating back to the 16th century. The room was used during the time of the 4th Earl to meet and discuss politics – he was a leading Conservative and member of Disraeli's cabinet in the 1860s and 1870s. The Earl of Grantham uses it in *Downton Abbey* for a similar purpose – it is here that he discusses the workings of the estate with his butler, interviews his Irish chauffeur, Branson, before employment and also uses the room as a retreat, often sitting at his writing desk. The current Carnarvon family likes to use the library to meet before and after meals.

Countess Almina received bolts of fine green French silk from her father Alfred de Rothschild in 1895 as a wedding gift, and used them to decorate the walls of the south-facing drawing room. The re-discovered Egyptian artefacts were hidden in the narrow cupboards between the double doors leading from the drawing room to the smoking room. The latter contains Dutch paintings dating from the 17th century and works of art collected on the Grand Tour of Europe in the early 19th century. The morning room, adjacent to the study and the original drawing room before the remodelling, is said to be used by Dame Maggie Smith and Penelope Wilton to relax in between takes.

[The Arundel bedroom]

Only the first floor and, of course, the ground floor of the house can be accessed by visitors. Several of the bedrooms make an appearance in *Downton Abbey* – the Stanhope room, decorated in rich red as it was for the 1895 visit by the Prince of Wales, became Lady Mary's bedroom, in which the Turkish diplomat Kemal Pamuk rather inconveniently dies of a heart attack while making amorous advances on her, his body then having to be removed from her bed. The Mercia bedroom, with its four-poster bed, 18th century silks and furniture from the same period, doubled as Lady Cora's bedroom. Finally the Arundel bedroom and its adjoining dressing room were two of the rooms converted by Countess Almina into the Operating Theatre and Recovery Room. As the series continued it became more convenient to build studio sets of the bedrooms, certainly when scenes such as the fire in Lady Edith's bedroom in episode 5.1 had to be filmed.

41

About 100 years ago, the castle would have employed sixty staff, including a house steward, butlers, footmen, housekeepers, maids and kitchen staff. The stairs hidden behind the green baize doors of the saloon, connecting the whole house, were used by the servants; at the bottom are the former staff dining room, the cellars and kitchens. The staff would have been alerted to the requirements upstairs by way of a bell system, installed in 1895 – a bell would ring, each room's bell with a slightly different tone, a red disc would then indicate the room from which it had been rung. The servants' rooms shown in the television programme however are not filmed at Highclere – the stairs were partially recreated by the television crew at Ealing Studios (page 82). Today the stairs lead the visitor to the Egyptian exhibition in the basement, and fewer staff are employed in the house, including a real-life butler and a chef, alongside forty tour guides for the visitors.

The chef almost copied a storyline from the series, albeit involuntarily – he woke up one day and couldn't see anything in one eye. His doctor could not find what the issue was, so Lady Carnarvon paid for him to visit a consultant, who found that the chef had had a stroke, just as Lady Grantham pays for Mrs. Patmore's eye problem to be attended to at Moorfields Eye Hospital (page 71) in episode 1.7. The chef joked, that after copying a further storyline involving an incorrect recipe for Apple Charlotte, he wouldn't mind imitating one in which the cook wins the lottery!

The Carnarvon family and their guests use either the 'oak staircase' or the 'red staircase'. The former took a year to carve and install into the tall Italianate tower, while the latter leads to the old nursery rooms on the second floor.

Between 1774 and 1777 in reconstructing the park to the designs of Capability Brown, the 1st Earl relocated the village of Highclere. The remains of the original village church dating back to 1689 can be found at the south-west corner of the castle.

Several follies adorn the grounds. Jackdaws Castle was built in 1743 by Robert Herbert, using Corinthian columns from Berkeley House in London, which had burnt down in 1733. Then there is Heaven's Gate, an eighteen metre tall structure erected in 1731 on Sidown Hill. The careful observer will be able to spot both of these buildings in the background of various shots throughout the series. But the most impressive folly overlooks Duns Mere in Highclere Park, some distance from the house. This is the Temple of Diana, which has been restored by the 8th Earl of Carnarvon with financial support from various interested organisations. It is into this lake, with the temple on the hill behind, that Bates, assisted by Mrs. Hughes, throws his limp corrector into the water, never to be seen again.

[Jackdaws Castle (top) and the Temple of Diana (bottom)]

Also worthy of note are the Lebanon Cedar trees in the garden, which were grown from seeds brought back during the 18th century by the seed collector Bishop Stephen Pococke. The cedar tree on the front lawn was the setting for the garden party in the last episode of series one, when Matthew Crawley decides not to marry Lady Mary, and the Earl informs all assembled of the outbreak of World War I.

The gardens at Highclere Castle were first recorded in 1218, but are certainly older: the Monks' Garden, which derives from the Bishop's palace, is very likely the oldest part. No vegetables are grown in the gardens today, but peaches and nectarines are cultivated in the glasshouse, along with tea roses for the decoration of the big house. Along the walls of the Monks' Garden, different fruit trees are trained. The present Earl has had fifteen thousand bulbs planted in the gardens to date. Please note that, although there are public footpaths and seasonal walks, the gardens and woods can be explored only when Highclere Castle is open to the general public.

[Mr. Crump's smithy is also on the Highclere estate]

Other parts of the estate will also look familiar to *Downton Abbey* viewers. For example it will be recalled that in episode 1.5 Lady Sybil, in her encouragement of Gwen to find a secretarial position, applies for a job on her behalf, and to her delight obtains an interview. They sneak off together by horse and cart, but all does not go to plan, as the horse casts a shoe and is in need of a blacksmith. On enquiring from a man walking a dog (at the humpback bridge which cars pass over when leaving the estate) they are told to "try old Crump in the next village", but on arrival find that Mr. Crump is away all week working at another estate. The smithy is actually one of the disused farm buildings located at the northern part of Highclere Park.

[Local club cricket is very much still a feature at Highclere]

Not far from Mr. Crump's smithy is the location of Downton cricket pitch, which features so prominently in the last episode of series three, when Thomas so very nearly gets arrested by the police for homosexuality.

The area around Highclere has been referred to in *The Tatler* as Downtonia. Filming for *Downton Abbey* usually takes place in the spring before the estate opens to the general public for the three summer months (as well as some selected dates in the pre-Christmas season). The castle does offer private tours for small groups and also fine dining. In addition Highclere has hosted a number of celebrity weddings, as for example in 2005 when Katie Price (Jordan) and Peter Andre were married here.

As a direct consequence of the television series visitor numbers to the estate have increased by 30-40%, making Highclere probably the most recognised stately home in the world at present. In the aftermath of the first series airing on television, Highclere took no fewer than six hundred coach bookings during the summer – compared to just one hundred the year before. However, visitor numbers have to be limited to protect the house and its contents. It is highly recommended that tickets should be booked in advance due to the estate's popularity. If you intend to visit Highclere please refer to the web site first (www.highclerecastle.co.uk).

Finally it isn't just *Downton Abbey* that has been filmed here, for Highclere has appeared in many other productions, the most notable being *The Missionary* (1982), *The Secret Garden* (1987), *King Ralph* (1991), *Robin Hood: Prince of Thieves* (1991), *Eyes Wide Shut* (1999) and *The Four Feathers* (2002), while on the small screen it can be spotted in *Jeeves and Wooster* (6 episodes) and as the setting for the 2004 *Agatha Christie Marple* episode *4.50 from Paddington* with Geraldine McEwan.

[Burghclere's Portal Hall which doubles as Downton School]

Burghclere is the site of Beacon Hill, which overlooks the Highclere Estate, from where various panoramic shots have been taken. It is also the location of Portal Hall, which dates to 1889 and was built in memory of Canon Portal on land given by the Earl of Canarvon. The hall appears as Downton School in both series 5 and 6, and is, of course, where Miss. Bunting, and later, Mr. Molesley work, and where Daisy Mason takes her matriculation exam. But it is most memorable as the place where Charles Carson and Elsie Hughes hold their wedding celebrations in episode 6.3.

46

DOWNTON ABBEY IN KENT

CHATHAM - THE HISTORIC DOCKYARD CHATHAM

[The Historic Dockyard Chatham buildings provide a perfect setting for the Ripon Union Workhouse]

The name Chatham, first recorded in 880 as Cetham, probably derives from a pre-Saxon root indicating a settlement in a valley or river-basin. People have dwelt there since Roman times, as the town stands on the ancient road that the Saxons later named Watling Street, the route now followed by the main A2 from London to Dover. For centuries Chatham was no more than a quiet village beside the River Medway, but in the 16th century its strategic possibilities as a port were recognised, and warships were harboured there. It became a Royal Dockyard in 1569 during the reign of Queen Elizabeth I, initially just for repairs but then as a shipbuilding yard. Perhaps the most famous vessel launched here was HMS Victory, on the 7th May 1765 (although she did not leave Chatham for sea service until 1778). After World War I the dockyard concentrated on submarine building, with some fifty-seven being built between 1908 and 1960.

Around the dockyard various fortifications were built to defend the town from attack. Upnor Castle was built in 1567, but proved ineffectual when the Dutch made a raid on the Medway in 1667. This resulted in a whole complex of forts being constructed, including Fort Amherst which today is a major visitor attraction in the area. By the middle of the 19th century Chatham was surrounded by three rings of forts, including Fort Pitt (which shortly became a hospital and then the original home of the Army Medical School), Fort Luton, Fort Bridgewood and Fort Borstal. The soldiers and sailors who manned the forts were stationed at Kitchener Barracks, the

Royal Marine Barracks, Brompton Artillery Barracks, Melville Barracks, and the naval barracks at HMS Collingwood and HMS Pembroke.

Chatham's most famous resident was Charles Dickens, who later described his time there as the happiest years of his childhood. In 1856 he returned to the area, buying Gad's Hill Place in nearby Higham, where he lived until his death in 1870.

The whole area was a hive of activity until after World War II, when the importance of the dockyard began to decline. In 1984 it closed altogether with the loss of around seven thousand civilian jobs, representing almost a quarter of the town's adult population. What now remains is a stunning eighty-acre site (out of an original four hundred acres) with historic buildings, museum galleries and historic warships, along with a vibrant programme of events and activities. The highlights include three historic warships (HMS Gannet, HMS Cavalier and the submarine HMS Ocelot), the Victorian ropery (a grade I listed building in which you can experience life as a rope maker and take a costumed guided tour), the wooden walls of England (an award-winning reconstruction of the dockyard of the Age of Sail), the historic lifeboat collection of seventeen vessels, and finally 3 Slip – The Big Space (containing such diverse exhibits as a Midget submarine, giant tools and steam machinery, Kitchener's railway carriage, the D-Day locomotive 'Overlord', mine-clearing equipment and a huge Chieftain tank). For further details see www.thedockyard.co.uk.

The Kent Film Office makes great play of the fact that filming was done here for the James Bond film *The World Is Not Enough* (1999), but the actual scene lasts just a few seconds, and purports to be London. Other productions filmed here include *The Golden Compass* (2007), *Amazing Grace* (2007), *The Mummy* (1999), *Sherlock Holmes* (2009) and *Les Misérables* (2012), while on the small screen *Foyle's War*, *Vanity Fair*, *Tipping the Velvet*, *Mill on the Floss*, *A Christmas Carol*, *Canterbury Tales* and most recently *Call The Midwife* and *Mr. Selfridge* have all been on location here.

For *Downton Abbey* the Tarred Yarn Store appears in episode 4.1 as the Ripon Union Workhouse where Charles Grigg, one half of the 'Cheerful Charlies', now spends his days. Mrs Hughes finds him here in reduced circumstances and takes pity on him after Mr. Carson refuses to help. Eventually Isobel Crawley rescues him from the workhouse and takes him into her own house until he is on his feet again, eventually getting a job in Belfast and exiting the series for good.

Tenterden - Kent & East Sussex Railway

[The home of England's first light railway is Tenterden Town]

The Ashford to Hastings railway line had originally been planned to pass through Tenterden, but Parliament preferred a more southerly route. Tenterden had a second chance of getting a railway station in 1855 when a line from Headcorn via Cranbrook was proposed (and rejected), and a third in 1864 with another proposal for a line from Paddock Wood via Cranbrook and Tenterden to Hythe (also rejected).

It was only with the passing of the Light Railways Act of 1896, which allowed for cheaper construction methods in return for speed restrictions, that Tenterden was to get a station. Under the Act the rails used had to be of at least 60 pounds per yard in weight, with the maximum speed allowed being 15 miles per hour (later raised to 25 miles per hour). The first passenger train ran on the 2nd April 1900, but it could not really be said to serve Tenterden, since the station (later renamed Rolvenden Parkway) was some two miles from the town. An extension to Tenterden Town station was opened on the 15th May 1905.

Interestingly, after World War I the railway was not taken over by one of the 'Big Four' but continued its independent existence. The Southern Railway (under whose auspices the railway would have fallen) was probably quite relieved, since the line seldom made a profit. In 1932

William Henry Austin was appointed the Official Receiver. He tried to sell off worn out stock to the Southern Railway in order to obtain enough money to hire serviceable rolling stock from them in return. One batch of stock, valued at £855, realised less than £7. However, his efforts were enough for the railway did keep running, though its finances remained precarious. During World War II some railway mounted guns were stationed at Rolvenden and Wittersham, and the line was also used as an alternative route to the coast. At nationalisation in 1948 the line became part of Southern Region. Some improvements were made, but the passenger numbers did not increase, and in consequence the last scheduled passenger service ran on the 2nd January 1954.

Preservation activities started immediately, but it was not until 1974 that the line partially re-opened between Tenterden Town and Rolvenden. This was followed by extensions to Wittersham Road (1977), Northiam (1990) and Bodiam (2000). Currently there are plans afoot to link up with the Rother Valley Railway at Robertsbridge, meaning that once again Tenterden would become connected to the mainline.

[Terrier 32678, presently in British Railways livery, as seen in the opening shots of *Downton Abbey*]

The Terrier class locomotive seen in the very opening shot of the very first episode of *Downton Abbey* is No. 78 Knowle. Unfortunately this is totally out of place for a train in Yorkshire, as this particular engine emerged from the Brighton Works in July 1880 as part of the last batch of A1 class locomotives. At first, Knowle worked on the London suburban lines, but by the mid-1890s had migrated to Portsmouth, working the Hayling Island and East Southsea branches.

In 1907 it was renumbered 678 by the London, Brighton & South Coast Railway (the number is clearly visible in *Downton Abbey*), and that same year it was converted to a push-pull motor train, whereby the locomotive could be controlled from a driver's position in a trailer carriage. This avoided the problem on a single track of having to run the locomotive round its coaches at the end of each trip. The adaptation included reducing the cylinders from 13 inches to 12 inches in diameter: as a consequence Knowle has rather less power, although still adequate for duties on a light railway. By November 1911 Knowle had clocked 763,993 up miles. In 1912 the engine was allocated to Horsham, moving to Littlehampton four years later and then returning to the London area, where its duties included the Crystal Palace motor trains. By the end of 1922 Knowle was back in the country, at Horsham.

It is believed that when the network was taken over by the Southern Railway the locomotive was stored out of use at Preston Park from 1926 until 1929, when, in May of that year, it was shipped across the Solent to become Isle of Wight W4 Bembridge (W14 from 1932). Its Island duties came to an end in May 1936, and it returned to the mainland, only to be condemned at Eastleigh seven months later. However a reprieve was granted and, after an overhaul, it returned to traffic in May 1937 as No. 2678, going to Fratton for duty on the Hayling Island services. A year later it was tried as shed pilot at Guildford but found to be unsuitable.

During World War II it was loaned to the Kent & East Sussex Railway, as a temporary measure to alleviate a chronic motive power shortage. It remained on loan until nationalisation in 1948 and was then retained for service on the line for another ten years (being renumbered 32678 in 1949). It ran on the day of the final scheduled passenger service in 1954, after which it moved to St. Leonards for freight duties (and for the seasonal hop-pickers' trains). This lasted until 1958 when diesels took over the freight trains. Its final days were spent at Fratton for the Hayling Island branch duties, the West Quay line at Newhaven until that closed on the 10th August 1962, and then as a coal stage pilot at Brighton, before being withdrawn from service on the 5th October 1963 (at which time the total mileage recorded was 1,411,436). Luckily the engine was bought the following year by Butlin's, who put it on display at their Minehead holiday camp. From there it was moved to the West Somerset Railway, and then back to the Kent & East Sussex Railway, where it arrived in kit form in 1988. It re-entered service in May 1999.

**[One of the vintage train carriages used to take Bates to
Downton Abbey in the first episode of the first series]**

The train conveying Bates comprises Knowle, two coaches (a 6-wheeler
and a 4-wheeler) and some freight wagons: i.e. a mixed traffic train, which
would have been quite correct for a rural branch line serving somewhere
like Downton. The coaches, which are from the right period, had false
panels added to indicate that they belonged to the North East Railway.
Today these coaches form part of the 'vintage train' at the Kent & East
Sussex Railway and see regular service. All the other railway scenes to date
have used Horsted Keynes station at the neighbouring Bluebell Line in
West Sussex (page 188)

Most of the preserved railways are popular locations for filmmakers, and
the Kent & East Sussex Railway is no exception. It should be familiar to
readers from films such as *Dracula* (1973), *Flame* (1974), *Nineteen Eighty-
Four (*1984*), *Cold Comfort Farm* (1995) and *Jude* (1996), while on the
small screen it can be spotted in, amongst others, *We'll Meet Again*,
Partners in Crime, *Dempsey and Makepeace*, *The Charmer*, *The Darling
Buds of May* and *The Woman in White*.

The Kent & East Sussex Railway, which bills itself as 'England's first light
railway', is certainly one of the best preserved of all the heritage lines in
the country, with over 11 miles of track. One of its most popular attractions
is the Wealden Pullman dining trains, for which early booking is advised.
Tenterden makes a great family day out, but visitors are advised to check
the railway web site (www.kesr.org.uk) first for timetables, prices and
details of special events.

DOWNTON ABBEY IN LINCOLNSHIRE

LINCOLN - LINCOLN CASTLE

[The East Gate of Lincoln Castle became the entrance to York Prison in *Downton Abbey*]

Lincolnshire, bordered by Norfolk, Cambridgeshire, Rutland, Leicestershire, Nottinghamshire, South Yorkshire, the East Riding of Yorkshire and Northamptonshire (for just 18 metres – the shortest county boundary in England), was formed when the ancient kingdom of Lindsey

53

merged with the lands controlled by the Danelaw borough of Stamford. Later the name Lindsey came to refer only to the northern part of the county around the city of Lincoln.

Remains survive of an Iron Age settlement where the Romans later built the town called Lindum, from which the Fosse Way led to Exeter and Ermine Street led to York. It was established around the legionary fortress, on a hill overlooking Brayford Pool, the natural lake formed by the widening of the River Witham. When the legion moved on to York in A.D. 71 the town became known as Lindum Colonia, signifying a settlement for army veterans. The colony flourished, being accessible from the sea via the Rivers Trent and Witham (to connect the two rivers, the Romans constructed the Fossdyke, believed to be the oldest canal in England still in use), but by the 5th century the town was largely deserted. Even before the Romans had departed there were raids by Picts and Scots, the first as early as 367. In the 6th century the Angles and Saxons invaded from Germany, sweeping the former Romano-Celtic inhabitants westwards, and in about 584 the kingdom of Mercia was founded, apparently by two formerly rival tribes. The stability this brought to the region lasted until 839, when the Vikings sailed up the River Witham and laid waste the city. Although they did not stay long then, they returned in greater numbers in 865 and settled in the area, where their colony became one of the Five Boroughs at the heart of the Danelaw. Rule of the Five Boroughs was retaken by the English during 916 and 917, under Edward the Elder, son of Alfred the Great. King Olaf of York reoccupied the Boroughs in 941, but King Edmund conquered them again the following year. In 1016, when Canute the Dane became undisputed King of England, he brokered a lasting agreement between the Danes and the English.

By the time of the Norman Conquest the population of Lincoln was around 12,000, putting it on a par with York. There were no fewer than four churches within the boundary of the Roman fort, and up to eighteen within the city. In 1068 William the Conqueror ordered a castle to be built in Lincoln, opposite the cathedral, which had been under construction since 1062. By the time the spire was added to the central tower in the early 14th century it was said to be the tallest building in the world (alas, the spire was blown down in the middle of the 16th century). It is interesting to note that in 1068 the constable of the castle was Coleswain, a man of Saxon origins, who had a garrison of only sixteen men, whereas Bishop Remigius, a Norman, had forty-five men to guard the cathedral.

Lincoln Castle played a pivotal role during the Civil War between the Empress Matilda, also called Maud, and King Stephen. Just before Christmas 1140 Matilda's army, under the command of Ranulph, Earl of

Chester and William de Roumare, captured the castle. An enraged Stephen attacked the castle once again, but Ranulph, being warned, was able to summon help from Robert, Earl of Gloucester, and in the ensuing Battle of Lincoln, on the 2nd February 1141, Stephen was captured and taken to Bristol, where he was imprisoned. However, this was not the end of the conflict. Stephen was subsequently exchanged for the Earl of Gloucester, who had been captured in the Rout of Winchester in September 1141, and the hostilities continued. In 1143, in another attempt to besiege the castle, Stephen tried to tunnel under the walls, but the tunnel caved in, killing eighty of his men. Three years later he invited Ranulph to Northampton for peace talks, but instead arrested him and threatened to execute him unless he surrendered Lincoln. He did so, and Christmas 1147 saw Stephen's court at the castle. The next year Matilda gave up her claim to the English throne and returned to France. Ranulph's estates in France were restored to him by Stephen, and he retained the Lucy Tower at Lincoln Castle and the title Earl of Lincoln. Victory was short-lived, however. Ranulph died in December 1153 after drinking poisoned wine, and upon Stephen's death in October 1154, Matilda's son became King Henry II.

Henry had the castle defences improved, replacing the old timber stockade with stone walls, building stone keeps on top of both mottes, and strengthening the gateways. After Henry came Richard I, who left the administration of his kingdom to William Longchamps, Bishop of Ely, being more interested in fighting in the Holy Land. Longchamps sold Lincoln Castle to Gerard de Camville, a supporter of Prince John, who in turn challenged the authority of Longchamps. After unsuccessfully laying siege to the castle, the bishop fled to France, and in 1199 John became king. The year after John had set his seal to Magna Carta in 1215, war broke out with the French - and with a number of barons intent on replacing the King with Prince Louis, son of the French king. Although Louis took control of London, the troops he sent to take Lincoln were rebuffed, and the siege crumbled with the onset of winter. Another French attempt to seize Lincoln culminated in the second Battle of Lincoln (also known as the Battle of Lincoln Fair) on the 20th May 1217. The French, having taken up poor defensive positions within the city walls, were driven back into the area between the castle and cathedral, where they were easy targets for the English archers. They retreated to the water meadows just as reinforcements from the Earl of Chester arrived, and the result was a massacre. Louis fled to France, never to return or to lay claim to the English throne again.

The remainder of the 13th century saw prosperous times for Lincoln. The town became one of the four largest in England, the main produce being wool, mostly woven into cloth and dyed. Robin Hood's merry men famously wore Lincoln green.

In 1311 ownership of the castle passed to the earls of Lancaster. The 4th Earl, created Duke of Lancaster in 1351, died without male issue, but his daughter Blanche married Prince John of Gaunt, King Edward III's fourth son, who was created Duke of Lancaster in 1362. Lincoln castle became part of the Duchy of Lancaster, which merged with the crown in 1399 when John's son became King Henry IV. (In 1831 an Act of Parliament allowed the city justices to purchase the castle from the Duchy for £2,000.) By that time the Black Death had killed off around half the population, leaving insufficient manpower to keep the River Witham navigable. Trade moved downstream to Boston, and Lincoln became a literal backwater for the next four centuries. At the outbreak of the English Civil War Lincoln was firmly allied to Cromwell, but the city was of strategic importance to both sides and changed hands several times. After the Battle of Winceby in 1643, a decisive victory for Parliament, the royalists abandoned Lincoln. They were in control again by March but were defeated in May after a three day siege by the Earl of Manchester. In 1648 Lincoln was again taken by the royalists. The parliamentary soldiers were soon forced to surrender, but not before they had set fire to the Bishop's palace, where they had taken refuge. In turn the royalists fled when a relieving army under Colonel Rossiter was spotted. This was the last conflict for the city, which thereafter became more of a quiet rural market town.

Weekly trials were held in the medieval hall of the castle, with more serious cases being decided at the twice-yearly assizes, which also took place in the great hall until 1776, when a dedicated court was built. Unfortunately it was affected by subsidence, and was replaced in 1826 by Robert Smirke's gothic revival building. Also within the castle bailey was the gaol, dating from 1787 and enlarged in 1844-8. Today it looks much as it did in 1878, when it was abandoned in favour of a new building in Greetwell Road. Public hangings (a total of thirty-eight are recorded) took place outside the north-west corner of the bailey, usually at noon on Fridays, market day, when a large crowd would be on hand to watch the spectacle. Public executions ceased in 1868, and until 1877 hangings were carried out on a portable gallows erected in the prison yard close to the south wall of the court building. A unique surviving feature is the chapel, where each prisoner, wearing a leather mask, was separated from his neighbours by tall wooden screens. Once the prisoners were seated, an officer would operate a mechanism to secure the screens in place, preventing any contact between them. The only person they could see was the chaplain in his pulpit. The so-called 'separate system' of punishment was intended to strip each inmate of his identity and eradicate any sort of conspiracy. At the rear of the chapel a row of open seats was reserved for condemned prisoners, who were thought to be beyond redemption.

[The first floor landing where Bates resided in one of the cells on the left hand side. Note that a couple of the covers to the modern strip lighting are now missing]

Lincoln Castle has appeared in several television productions, such as the pilot for the series *Diamond Geezer*, and was more recently the subject of a

Time Team investigation. Most notably, however, this is where John Bates was imprisoned in *Downton Abbey*. In the series, of course, it doubled as York prison, with prop signage to make the setting plain. The upper floor of the men's prison and the landing area featured most prominently, along with the East Gate, which served as the prison entrance, and the Eastern Courtyard, since excavated, which became the exercise yard. Besides the signs, the art department also had to construct covers for the modern strip lighting and wall sockets, and even some cell doors.

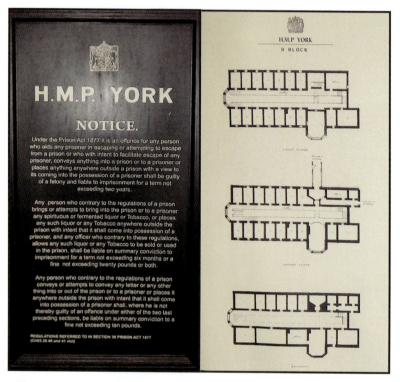

[Some of the prop signage used is still in evidence at Lincoln Castle]

Interestingly, when Anna Smith arrives by motor car outside the prison gate on Castle Hill to pick up Bates upon his release, we see him walking towards the gate from the wrong side. He is actually already on the outside, heading towards the gaol, with Anna behind him! (Perhaps he had read the script for the next episode and decided that it was safer to remain inside …) The gate he emerges from is actually a prop, erected behind the East Gate next to what is now the souvenir shop. The various prison scenes were all filmed back to back over a two week period.

[Polystyrene mouldings were used to cover modern electrical sockets (left) while it was easier to make false cell doors rather than re-hang the originals (right)]

[Recent excavations have lowered the level of the exercise yard]

[The warders' office next to which the prisoners line up to collect their mail (top) and the corridor leading from the cell block which Bates is seen to pass down just prior to his release (bottom)]

The castle was first opened to the public in 1884, when it became a popular attraction, with people coming from far afield to view the city from the towers and battlements. Today the castle is open throughout the year, closing only for Christmas and New Year celebrations. At certain times of the year, the entrance fee also includes a free guided tour. At present, because of the Lincoln Castle Revealed project, which is carrying out vital restoration to the south and east curtain walls, there is limited access to some parts of the castle. The Lucy Tower and the Observation Tower are both currently closed to the public, as is the prison itself, due to the excavations in the Eastern Courtyard. However, there is a viewing platform for the public to watch the ongoing work. For further details see www.lincolnshire.gov.uk/lincolncastle.

DOWNTON ABBEY IN LONDON

London, on the River Thames, is the largest city, urban zone and metropolitan area in the United Kingdom, and also Europe by most criteria. It has been a major settlement for over two thousand years with a history going back to Roman times, when it was called Londinium. The City of London still retains many of its medieval boundaries, and many curious traditions. The official population of London is just over eight million persons, although if the metropolitan areas are also included this number rises to somewhere between twelve and fourteen million, or one fifth of the population of the United Kingdom.

Today London is a global centre for the arts, commerce, education, entertainment, fashion, finance, healthcare, media, professional services, research and development, tourism and transport. It is hardly surprising that production crews see the city as just one big film set. Even in a production such as *Downton Abbey* set in Yorkshire some of the characters inevitably visit the capital, while many of the indoor scenes are in fact stage sets at Ealing Studios. It must be remembered that London is where all the major film and television studios in the country are located, and for this reason it is to places within an hour's travel of these studios that production companies travel for location filming.

For the purposes of this guide locations used are presented alphabetically by the closest Underground/Overground station.

BARBICAN - CHARTERHOUSE
CHARTERHOUSE SQUARE

World War II outdid the damage of the Great Fire of London, with the Guildhall and everything around it to the north between Aldersgate and Moorgate (some 35 acres) being completely burnt out and laid waste. This was the area now known as Barbican. It was noted that 'one could walk for over half a mile without passing a single standing structure'.

To the west of Barbican is Smithfield, originally Smoothfield, described in the middle ages as 'a plain grassy space just outside the City Walls'. Here, as Thomas Becket's clerk William FitzStephen wrote in 1173, 'every Friday there is a celebrated rendezvous of fine horses to be sold,' and it seems that sheep, pigs and cattle were also traded. In 1400 the City of London was granted the tolls from the market by charter.

From 1123 until its suppression in 1855 for rowdiness and debauchery, Smithfield was the site of the famous Bartholomew Fair. As a convenient open area close to the City, it was also used for tournaments, jousting and sporting events. A tournament held in 1357 was attended by the Kings of both England and France.

Between Barbican and Smithfield, on the south side of Charterhouse Square, is Carthusian Street, which runs westward into Charterhouse Street, the northern boundary of Smithfield Market. On the north side of the square is the Charterhouse, formally Sutton's Hospital in Charterhouse.

[Master's Court where Branson first tells Lady Sybil of his affections for her while watching the wounded soldiers exercise]

In 1348-9 Sir Walter de Manny, one of King Edward III's bravest knights, bought 13 acres of land adjoining Pardon Churchyard, part of which he gave to the City as a burial ground for victims of the Black Death. He built a small chapel where Charterhouse Square now is. In 1370, on the remaining land, Manny established a Carthusian monastery, originally of just eight monks in temporary accommodation. The following year the House of Salutation of the Mother of God, better known as Charterhouse, received its foundation charter. By the end of the year the first 'cells' (two-storey houses in their own garden) were ready. Each had a workroom, oratory, bedroom, living-room and wood-store.

In 1535 the heads of the three English Carthusian monasteries, including Prior John Houghton of the Charterhouse, pleaded with Thomas Cromwell

(Earl of Essex and a chief minister to King Henry VIII) for their houses to be exempt from the new Act of Supremacy. Instead they were arrested, and on 4th May were hanged at Tyburn, and, while still alive, cut down and quartered, for 'treacherously machinating and desiring' to deprive the King of his title as Supreme Head of the Church. Ten monks of the Charterhouse were sent to Newgate Prison, nine of whom starved to death in gaol. The tenth was later executed at Tower Hill. In 1537 the monastery was dissolved and the property and handed to the King, who used it for storing hunting equipment. It was subsequently granted to Lord North, who constructed a fine Tudor mansion on the site.

In November 1558 Queen Elizabeth I stayed here for five nights leaving to spend a vigil at the Tower of London before her coronation. She stayed again for three nights in July 1561, but the expense nearly bankrupted Lord North, who was forced to retire to the country. In 1565 Thomas Howard, 4th Duke of Norfolk, purchased Charterhouse, renaming it Howard House, but his scheme to marry Mary Queen of Scots resulted in imprisonment in the Tower of London and eventual execution in 1572. After a quick succession of occupants, including the Portuguese Ambassador and the Earl of Cumberland, the house became the property of Norfolk's second son, Thomas Howard, 1st Earl of Suffolk and Admiral of the Fleet. Elizabeth was to stay here one final time in May 1603. Her successor, King James I, stayed for four days on his arrival in London, and created one hundred and thirty-three new knights in the great chamber, as well as making Suffolk his Lord Chamberlain.

Suffolk always preferred his house at Audley End, and in May 1611 he sold the London mansion for £13,000 to Thomas Sutton, known as the wealthiest commoner in England. At Charterhouse Sutton endowed a charitable foundation to educate boys and care for elderly men, known as 'Brothers'. There were places for forty-four boys and eighty poor gentlemen. Among those who were educated at Charterhouse before the school moved to Godalming in 1872 were Richard Lovelace, Richard Steele, John Wesley, Joseph Addison, Sir William Blackstone, John Leech, Lord Baden-Powell, General Havelock, Sir Johnston Forbes-Robertson and W. M. Thackeray.

The almshouses remained, though in 1941 considerable damage, subsequently restored, was done in an air raid. In 1949 the area to the east of the site became the Medical College of St. Bartholomew's Hospital; it is now occupied by Bart's and the London School of Medicine and Dentistry, Queen Mary, University of London. At Charterhouse today there is accommodation for forty Brothers, each having a bedroom and sitting room with en suite facilities, and a small kitchen. Once a Brother has entered he will be looked after for the rest of his life.

[Wash-house court showing the contrast between the early stonework to the right and later brickwork for the same building on the left. It was here that Lady Sybil was knocked unconscious during the counting of votes at the Ripon by-election]

Several parts of the Charterhouse have appeared in *Downton Abbey*. Wash-house Court is a quiet area that was originally the lay brothers' quarters. The court was evidently constructed in two stages, as the south and east ranges are of Kentish ragstone, while the west range, dating from 1531-32, is of brick, embellished with diaper work. The north wall is half stone and half brick, the decoration including diamond shapes and crosses. Also clearly visible are the letters I H, which may be the initials of John Houghton, or, as has been suggested, they may be all that remains of I H S, standing for *Iesus Hominum Salvator* (Latin for 'Jesus, Saviour of Men').

In episode 1.6 Lady Sybil, taking an interest in politics, attends a Liberal rally in Ripon, having been driven there by Branson. Later in the same episode, against the wishes of her father, she returns to Ripon and is present for the counting of votes at the by-election. The latter scene was shot in Wash-house Court.

**[Branson drives Lady Sybil under this arch on the way to the
counting of votes at the Ripon by-election]**

In that scene we see Branson driving the car from the direction of Entrance
Court toward Preacher's Court. He stops at the slype, the covered passage
to Wash-house Court, where Lady Sybil gets out and joins the crowd. An
anxious Branson tells her that he must park the car safely, but will return.

67

Next some agitators arrive, and a scuffle breaks out in which Lady Sybil is knocked unconscious to the ground. Luckily Matthew Crawley's offices are just around the corner, and he is on hand to rescue her and carry her off to safety, just as a knight in shining armour should.

[Another view of Ripon. This time it is Preacher's House that doubled as Matthew Crawley's workplace]

The geography here is actually quite correct, since the building used as the offices of Harvell and Carter, the solicitors for whom Matthew Crawley works, is in neighbouring Preacher's Court. The name comes from the preacher's house in the north-east corner, which is the building used in filming. The adjoining sections on the north, west and east sides of the court date from the late 1820s. The north range once had open cloisters, but these were blocked during World War II. However, in 2004 they were re-opened and glazed when the building was converted to become the Queen Elizabeth II Infirmary.

[The slype where Branson confesses]

The main courtyard in Lord North's time was Master's Court, reached via Entrance Court. Built in 1546, it has the great hall on the north side and the long gallery running the entire length of the first floor on the south side. To the east and west are Chapel Court and Wash-house Court. The great hall, with its tall windows, sundial and projecting bay, dominates the court, though it is rivalled by the lamp in the centre of the grassed area. Here, in the first episode of series 2, we see wounded soldiers exercising on the grass, while Branson tells Lady Sybil of his feelings for her in the slype.

Charterhouse Square itself is no stranger to filming. The Art Deco style block of flats on the east side, Florin Court, will be instantly recognised by many as the fictional Whitehaven Mansions, home of Hercule Poirot in the David Suchet television series. The building was constructed in 1936 by Guy Morgan and Partners, and is notable for its curved façade, roof garden and basement swimming pool. At the north-east corner of the square, Rutland Place leads to the Lodge House and the entrance to the medical campus for Queen Mary, University of London.

In the very first episode the door to the left of the early 15th century gateway to Entrance Court from Charterhouse Square became the front door of the Crawleys' town house in Manchester. Even for this simple exterior shot care had to be taken, with a restricted camera angle being used so that the sign for Charterhouse was not seen, and in addition a pillar box was added in front of the house to obscure 'no parking' signs on the railings (despite the fact that there actually was a double pillar box just out of shot to the right of the gateway).

[The door just to the left of the main gate to Charterhouse is the Crawleys' residence in Manchester]

No. 13 Charterhouse Square, situated on the left hand corner at the intersection with Rutland Place, is the former office of Bruce Gilbreth Architects. In episode 1.3 Bates is seen entering the basement of this building, which for the purposes of *Downton Abbey* is the premises of an artificial limb manufacturer. Bates's enquires about, and subsequently purchases, a limb corrector, which he hopes will cure his gammy leg and enable him to walk again without the need of a stick. In the event, sadly, it brings Bates no relief. In fact it makes things worse, causing him much pain in the process. Mrs. Hughes finally finds out about the device, and together she and Bates throw the contraption into the lake at Downton Abbey, never to be seen again (page 43).

**['Moorfields Eye Hospital' to the right and the basement shop where
Bates purchases his limb corrector to the left]**

The red-brick building on the right hand side as you proceed down Rutland
Place is Dean Rees House, which is now part of the medical campus. This
building was constructed in 1894 by W. Hilton Nash as lodgings for the
headmaster of the Merchant Taylors' School. In episode 1.7 of *Downton
Abbey*, it doubles as Moorfields Eye Hospital, where Mrs. Patmore goes to
have her cataract operation.

BOND STREET - THE SAVILE CLUB

Bond Street was built in two phases, Old Bond Street at the southern end,
between Piccadilly and Burlington Gardens, being the work of Thomas
Bond in 1684, and the rest of the street (New Bond Street) extending

71

northward to Oxford Street being the responsibility of the Corporation of London in the 1720s. The street was always pretty nondescript and as early as 1736 it was said that 'there is nothing in the whole prodigious length of the two Bond Streets ... that has anything worth our attention'.

It made its name, though, as a luxury shopping street, and in Georgian times it became a fashionable promenade for the *beau monde*, with shopkeepers renting part of their upper floors as lodgings. Among the residents of note were James Thomson (author of the words of *Rule Britannia*), Dean Swift, George Selwyn, Edward Gibbon, William Pitt the Elder, James Boswell and Admiral Nelson. Today the street is still fashionable and a centre for luxury goods such as jewellery, clothes, shoes and luggage. Companies to be found here include Asprey, Cartier Ltd., the Fine Art Society and, at Nos. 34-35 New Bond Street, Sotheby's.

Towards the Oxford Street end New Bond Street is crossed by Brook Street, which extends from Hanover Square to Grosvenor Square. The brook in question is the Tyburn River which flows beneath it at the intersection with Avery Row. Conversely to the 1736 description of the two Bond Streets, Brook Street was said to be 'for the most part nobly built and inhabited by people of quality' (as befits a *Downton Abbey* location). The 'quality' over the years includes George Frederick Handel (No. 25), William Pitt (No. 68), the architect William Shepherd (No. 72), Prime Minister Henry Addington (No. 47), the guitarist Jimmi Hendrix (No. 23) and Royal Physician, as well as one time Jack the Ripper suspect, Sir William Gull (No. 74). Also in the street is Claridge's, the 5-star hotel that most certainly would have been known to the Crawley family.

No. 69 Brook Street is a four-bay frontage with a garden and a mews which has since 1927 been home to the Savile Club (along with the adjacent No. 71). The club was founded in 1868 and first occupied rooms in the Medical Club at Trafalgar Square when it was known as the New Club. The present named dates from 1891 when it moved to a house in Savile Row. Membership is drawn largely from the arts and has included members as diverse as Herbert Spencer, Frank Muir and Sir Ralph Richardson. In *A Handful of Dust* Evelyn Waugh says that the club (referred to as the Greville) has 'a tradition of garrulity'.

As far as filming is concerned the building can be seen on the big screen in *Finding Neverland* (2004) while on television it has played host to the detectives Poirot, Campion and Inspector Lynley. For *Downton Abbey* a five-minute key sequence was filmed on the staircase and in the ballroom lobby when it doubled for the Lotus Club in London.

[The ballroom lobby which became the Lotus Club]

Indeed the lobby and staircase are the most spatially exciting part of the building. The Imperial stair, with its painted wooden balusters and moulded handrail, lead to the lobby which has wood panelling where can be found four paintings representing the four seasons on canvas glued on wood and set in moulded surrounds. The doors (one pair being faux doors) are adorned with either fretwork decoration or are mirrored. The room is large enough for a small orchestra to be set up, just as it was for *Downton Abbey*, or, for example, when Queen Mary dined here in 1924 when Cassano's orchestra provided the musical entertainment during dinner.

In episode 4.4 Lady Rose, Lady Mary, Tom Branson and Anna Bates are all staying at Lady Rosamund's house, when one night Lady Rosamund organises a surprise 'match-making' party at the Lotus Club where Lord Gillingham and Sir John Bullock, Rose's suitor of sorts are also in attendance. It is here that while dancing with Tony Gillingham that Lady Mary tells him that "I'm glad you came …" just before letting him down a few moments later with the words "I'm not ready …" and that it is time to "… go back to real life again", all while Jack Ross, the black bandleader sings *April Showers* on stage. Meanwhile Sir John, who is by now drunk and dancing with Lady Rose, causes a scene. It is Jack Ross who rescues her by leaving the stage and finishing the dance with the abandoned Lady Rose, much to Lady Rosamund's disapproval. The entrance hall also makes a brief appearance in episode 5.7 as the offices of *The Sketch* when Lady Rosamund, accompanied by the Countess of Grantham, visit Lady Edith.

CHARING CROSS - NATIONAL GALLERY
RULES RESTAURANT
SIMPSON'S-IN-THE-STRAND

The hamlet of Charing stood where the road from Bath to London turned north-west, following the direction of the River Thames. The name Charing comes from the Old English cierran, meaning to turn. When King Edward I's beloved wife, Eleanor of Castile, died in 1290 at Harby in Nottinghamshire, the funeral cortege rested at twelve places on the journey to Westminster Abbey, and a stone cross was erected at each, the last being the Charing Cross. It was made of Caen stone, with marble statues of the queen by Alexander of Abingdon, and stood at the top of Whitehall. In 1647, however, it was destroyed on the orders of Parliament, and some of the stone was used to pave the road. In 1675 the statue of King Charles I was erected on the same spot. Charing Cross is traditionally the heart of London. Distances are measured from here, and it has been said that anybody who wanted to know what was going on in London had merely to go to Charing Cross. Doctor Johnson remarked, 'I think the full tide of human existence is at Charing Cross'. The Eleanor Cross in the forecourt of Charing Cross station dates only from 1863; it was erected by the South Eastern Railway Company at a cost of £1,800.

[Trafalgar Square looking towards the National Gallery]

Along the length of the north side of Trafalgar Square is the National Gallery, which holds the national collection of old master paintings from the 13th century to the beginning of the 20th century. It was founded in 1824 when, during Lord Liverpool's government, the House of Commons voted £57,000 for the purchase of thirty-eight paintings, which had belonged to Russian-born merchant and banker John Julius Angerstein. The paintings were put on display at Angerstein's private house in Pall Mall. At this time two notable collectors, Sir George Beaumont and the Reverend Holwell

74

Carr, came forward offering their paintings for the nation if a suitable building could be found in which to display them. Other donations followed and the national collection soon had two hundred paintings by the likes of Correggio, Titian, Rubens, Rembrandt, Claude, Poussin, Reynolds, Hogarth and Lawrence.

In 1832 construction began on the present National Gallery, designed by William Wilkins, on the site of the King's Mews at Charing Cross, facing south over the newly created Trafalgar Square. The new building opened in 1838 was to increase gradually over the centuries with the growth of the collections. In 1876 a new wing, by E. M. Barry, was added, which includes the splendid dome room with its four chapels. The main staircase and five rooms beyond were a later addition by Sir John Taylor in 1887. With the opening of the Tate Gallery in 1897 most of the British and modern collections left Trafalgar Square, creating more space. In 1911 five more galleries were opened on the west side (where barracks once stood) to balance the Barry rooms on the east side. A northern extension on Orange Street was added in 1975, while the Sainsbury Wing was completed in 1999 to the west of the main building.

**[Interior of the National Gallery where three
Piero della Francesca paintings may be found]**

The pedestrianisation of Trafalgar Square resulted in the east wing scheme which allowed another public entrance from the square's north side. This had the advantage of providing a more direct route from the gallery's lower floor and more space for improved visitor facilities such as the shop and toilets. In 2005 the gallery had in its possession two thousand, three hundred works of art and a floor area equivalent to six football pitches. The National Gallery has free admission and is open daily from 10am to 6pm (9pm on Fridays) with the exception of the 1st January and 24th to 26th December when it is closed. For further details please visit www.nationalgallery.org.uk.

In *Downton Abbey* episode 5.3 the Countess of Grantham is being shown Piero della Francesca's *Nativity* by Simon Bricker. The picture is one of three by the artist that may be found at the National Gallery – the *Nativity* being located in Room 54 in the Sainsbury Wing. Piero is one of the most admired 15th century Italian painters. The cool colour palette and geometric compositions contribute to the refined and meditative nature of his works.

Just to the north-east of Charing Cross, running parallel to the Strand, is Maiden Lane, once part of an ancient track that ran through Covent Garden to St. Martin's Lane. It is thought to be named after a statue of the Virgin Mary that once stood at the street corner. The first houses were built there in about 1631, with more being added over the next century. Among the famous residents were the poet Andrew Marvell, and Voltaire, who lodged at the White Wig Inn during his exile from Paris. J. M. W. Turner was born here, in a room above his father's barber shop. Originally a dead end, Maiden Lane was made a through way so that Queen Victoria's carriage did not have to turn around after dropping her at the Adelphi Theatre.

At No. 35 Maiden Lane is Rules, the oldest restaurant in London, and one of the most famous. In 1798 Thomas Rule, having promised his family that he would forsake his feckless life and settle down in a steady business, opened what was then only an oyster bar in Maiden Lane. To the surprise of his relations the venture was a great success, quickly celebrated for its 'porter, pies and oysters', and frequented by 'rakes, dandies and superior intelligences'.

Until just before World War I the restaurant remained in the Rule family, but then an unusual transaction took place. Charles Rule, a descendant of the founder, met Tom Bell, owner of a Parisian restaurant called the Alhambra, and they agreed to swap restaurants. Rules was then run by the Bell family until 1984, when Tom Bell's daughter sold the establishment to the present owner, John Mayhew.

Rules is not only the oldest restaurant in London, it is one of the most celebrated in the world. It seats around one hundred and twenty persons over three floors, and employs over ninety staff who between them serve around one hundred and twenty thousand diners a year. The walls are covered with memorabilia, comprising paintings, prints, playbills and statuettes of its many distinguished patrons over the years.

[Rules proudly displays its royal warrant above the entrance]

Among the regular patrons were Charles Dickens, H. G. Wells and King Edward VII, who, when Prince of Wales was often accompanied by Lillie

Langtry. In fact the Prince and Mrs. Langtry were such frequent visitors that the restaurant had a private entrance installed so that they could go in and out unobserved. Others who have passed through the dining room include Henry Irving, Laurence Olivier, Buster Keaton, Charles Laughton, Clark Gable, Charlie Chaplin and Ava Gardner. Today's menu would still be recognisable to diners of the past, for house specialties include classic game, oysters, pies, puddings and occasionally Belted Galloway beef (a quality marbled beef from a heritage breed raised only on grass and hay) from the northern Pennine Hills.

[The table where Michael Gregson and Lady Sybil take lunch]

In episode 3.7 of *Downton Abbey* Lady Edith travels to London to meet the London editor of the weekly newspaper *The Sketch*, Michael Gregson (the character is based on Sir Bruce Ingram, who was actually the editor at this

78

time). He is determined to have her write a regular column for his newspaper, which was essentially a society magazine, focusing on royalty and the aristocracy. At a meeting at the newspaper offices Lady Edith promises to consider the proposal, adding that she has to visit the offices of *The Lady* on a family errand the next day before returning to Yorkshire. Gregson seizes the opportunity to invite her to lunch at Rules before taking the train home. For once the geography is quite correct, as the offices of *The Lady* magazine are in Bedford Street, only 100 metres or so from Rules. Over the meal, which was filmed at a table at the rear of the main restaurant, Lady Edith reveals that she was recently jilted at the altar, clearing the way for a possible romantic plot line to be developed. Later in the episode, over dinner at Downton Abbey, Edith announces, "Listen, everyone. You have a journalist in the family ..." to which the Dowager Countess quips, "Since we have a country solicitor, and a car mechanic, it was only a matter of time ..." A return visit is made in episode 5.8 when Lady Edith, Lady Mary and Tom Branson discuss what is to be done about the compromising photographs taken of Atticus Aldridge at his stag party. Its final appearance is in episode 6.3 as the place where Lady Edith and Bertie Pelham agree to have a drink. However, having just sacked her editor at *The Sketch* Lady Edith has a publication deadline to meet, and so rushes around the corner to Rules to tell Bertie that she can't have a drink with him. All ends happily as Bertie is only too pleased to help Lady Edith meet her deadline.

Rules has appeared in novels by Rosamond Lehmann, Evelyn Waugh, John Le Carré, Dick Francis and Graham Greene, who wrote: 'There are some restaurants which give one a sense of being at home, more at home than in a friend's house, welcome, at peace. Rules in Maiden Lane where I first went more than fifty years ago, is one. I even put it in a novel, *The End of the Affair'*. The Greene Room, one of the private dining areas, has on display letters and other memorabilia from Graham Greene and his sister, Elizabeth Dennys. Rules also makes an appearance in *Spectre* (2015) as the restaurant at which M, Q and Moneypenny eat and discuss how to help James Bond.

In 1818 Mr. Reiss opened 'a home for chess' in the Strand, which later became known as the Grand Cigar Divan (since the chess players sat on divans or sofas). Thirty years later John Simpson rebuilt the premises at which time it became Simpson's Divan and Tavern. He consulted Alex Soyer, the famous chef, and produced a menu of good roast beef and saddles of mutton which were served from a dinner wagon.

The building was demolished in 1900 when the Strand was widened, but it was rebuilt and opened in its present form in 1904 under the auspices of the

Savoy Hotel. Since then little has changed, and it is still renown for its roasts served at the table. Its patronage has included royalty from King George IV onwards as well as famous literary figures such as Charles Dickens, and it was even a favourite of Sherlock Holmes in the Arthur Conan Doyle stories.

[The entrance to Simpson's-in-the-Strand. Close inspection above the doors illustrates its chess heritage]

In episode 5.5 of *Downton Abbey* Lady Mary (who exclaims, "What a treat. I haven't been to Simpson's for ages.") and Charles Blake have dinner in the upper salon, only to find that Mabel Lane Fox is already seated at their table. It is all a scheme by Charles who hopes it will be "… as *The Times* advertisements say to your mutual advantage". The latter soon storms off, just before the beef trolley arrives, after realising that Charles is trying to get her and Lord Gillingham, who had broken off their engagement in favour of Lady Mary, back together again.

**[The Grand Divan at Simpson's-in-the-Strand, where Lady Mary
and Charles Blake have dinner]**

"But what shall we do with your food?" enquires Charles, to which Mabel
replies, "Eat it, and hope it chokes you". "Well that was a great success,"
comments Lady Mary, but actually it is far subtler than that, and as Charles
now declares, "… it was just a scene we had to play".

**[The entrance to the Grand Divan is most certainly
on the ground floor]**

81

The filming is not quite accurate since on entering the building the doors to the Grand Divan are clearly visible and closed. Next viewers see Lady Mary and Charles ascending the staircase to "… go straight in" to eat, but in the following shot they are clearly in the Grand Divan on the ground floor – such is the magic of television.

EALING BROADWAY - EALING STUDIOS

[The original entrance to Ealing Studios complete with Blue Plaque in honour of Michael Balcon to the right of the door]

The fact that this pretty nondescript part of West London is instantly associated with the film industry is due to Will Barker, who in 1907 bought a mansion in its own grounds and later added three glass stages for his film productions, close to what is now the site of Ealing Studios. His first film, *Henry VIII*, was made in 1911 and starred Sir Herbert Beerbohm Tree, who was paid the unheard-of sum of £1,000 a day. The film was a success, and other lavish (for the time) productions followed, which at their peak had up to one thousand extras. Barker was clever in also hiring out his facilities to other companies, so ensuring a regular income to offset any losses made by his own films.

In 1920 Barker retired and sold his enterprise to the General Film Renters Company, which promptly went out of business. In 1929 there was a new owner, Associated Radio Pictures Company, who invested money and built a new studio next to the existing ones. A.R.P. was successful in the 1930s, thanks largely to its two main stars, Gracie Fields and George Formby, who became Britain's highest paid actors of the time. The emphasis was now very much on entertainment and comedy and away from expensive lavish productions. Other stars who could be seen in Ealing at this time included Gloria Swanson, Laurence Olivier, Margaret Lockwood and even Ivor Novello, while David Lean, later a celebrated film director, worked here as an editor.

[The current main entrance (left) and reception (right) at the rather shabby Ealing Studios in west London]

It wasn't until 1938, and after several changes of management, that the complex became Ealing Studios, under the leadership of Michael Balcon. During his twenty years at the helm he was responsible for around ninety films, very few being box office disasters. This was the period of the celebrated 'Ealing Comedies', which became the hallmark of the studios, but not before another change of ownership in 1944, when the studios were bought out by the Rank Organisation. The output under Balcon included *Went the Day Well?* (1942), *Champagne Charlie* (1944), *Scott of the*

Antarctic (1948), *Whisky Galore* (1949), *Passport to Pimlico* (1949), *The Blue Lamp* (1950), *The Lavender Hill Mob* (1951) *The Man in the White Suit* (1951), *The Titfield Thunderbolt* (1953), *The Cruel Sea* (1953) and *The Ladykillers* (1955).

However, with the advent of television in the early 1950s the studios started to lose money and in 1955 the banks forced the owners to sell Ealing Studios for £300,000. The new owners, the B.B.C., never really made the fullest use of their asset, producing filmed inserts for such programmes as *Colditz* and *Porridge*, although some productions, such as *The Singing Detective* and *Fortunes of War*, were wholly shot here. In 1992 the B.B.C. sold Ealing Studios to the BBRK Group, but by 1994 that company was in receivership. In a complex deal Ealing Studios were then repurchased by the B.B.C. in 1995 and passed on to the National Film and Television School, but were sold again in 2000 to Uri Fruchtmann, Barnaby Thompson, Harry Handelsman and John Kao, who promised to revive the Studios as a film making concern. To their credit this is exactly what they have done. Recent productions have included *The Importance of Being Earnest* (2002), *Valiant* (2005), *Shaun of the Dead* (2004) and more recently the St. Trinian's franchise.

Today the Studios have three large sound stages, one small sound stage, two non-sound low-budget stages, a model stage, and water tank facilities. It is on the Ealing sound stages that many of the indoor scenes for *Downton Abbey* are shot, including, for example, the servants' hall and quarters, all re-created here at Ealing. The attention to detail is remarkable. The bell call system is fully operational, and controlled from various pulleys and levers behind the main board. Sadly, however, all the wonderful food cooked by Mrs. Patmore does not come from the large black stove in her kitchen, which is just painted wood. For a typical episode between a third and a half of all filming will be completed at Ealing Studios.

EMBANKMENT - WHITEHALL PLACE

There have been embankment schemes in London since Roman times, but the current one is a result of Sir Joseph Bazalgette's work on the main drainage system for London. He was the Chief Engineer of the Metropolitan Board of Works and responsible for overseeing over three-and-a-half miles of construction between 1868 and 1874 for what comprises the Albert, Victoria and Chelsea Embankments. They are the epitome of solid Victorian engineering with their thick parapets, occasional landing stages, granite block facing, rows of plane trees and iconic dolphin-based lamps of cast iron.

**[One Whitehall Place which doubled as the
entrance to the Grand Hotel, Liverpool]**

At the Charing Cross end such was the land reclamation that a new public area were formed at Whitehall Gardens, and just behind here, bounded by Whitehall Place, Whitehall Court and Horse Guards Avenue, is the eight storeys high block known as One Whitehall Place. It was built in the French Renaissance style in 1884 to the designs of Messrs Archer and Green. The building was home to many clubs in its time, but today only the Farmers' Club remains, though it is also the site for the National Liberal Club and the 376-bedroom Royal Horse Guards Hotel (officially at No. 2 Whitehall Place).

[Entrance and grand staircase at One Whitehall Place]

It is One Whitehall Place that Lady Mary can be seen entering in episode 5.2 of *Downton Abbey* when she is on her 'sketching trip', but is actually having a liaison with Lord Gillingham at the Grand Hotel, Liverpool. The porter's lodge doubles as the hotel reception, and after checking in Lady Mary is seen walking along the main entrance corridor and ascending the grand cantilever staircase (which was only built in 1950, the original having been destroyed by enemy action in 1941). The choice of location might seem strange for in the first place surely Lady Mary would not wish to be seen dead at the National Liberal Club, and second there is a perfectly good hotel adjacent. The staircase also makes a brief appearance in episode 5.3 as breakfast is served in bed, though the bedroom scenes are just a set back at Ealing Studios.

GREEN PARK - BRIDGEWATER HOUSE
LANCASTER HOUSE
RITZ HOTEL
ROYAL AUTOMOBILE CLUB

The park in question covers some 47 acres between Piccadilly and Constitution Hill. Unlike London's other Royal Parks, the area is given over almost entirely to grass and trees, without pretty flowerbeds, statuary or other ornamentation. Hence, of course, the name Green Park. Legend has it that the park was once the burial ground for the lepers from the Hospital of St. James, and that this explains the lack of flowers here compared to the adjoining St. James's Park (page 108). Green Park was enclosed by King Henry VIII and designated a Royal Park by King Charles II, who had the paths laid out and a snow house built for cooling drinks in the summer. The mound on which the snow house stood can still be seen opposite No. 119 Piccadilly.

During the 18th century the park was a favoured place for duelling, ballooning and firework displays. There was a particularly fine firework display here to celebrate the Peace of Aix-la-Chapelle of 1748, for which Handel composed the incidental music. The largest celebration, though, was in 1814 when a Gothic castle over thirty metres square was erected, with a grand fireworks display from the battlements. When the smoke had dissipated at the end of the fireworks the spectators saw a brightly illuminated Temple of Concord, its walls displaying allegorical pictures, prominent amongst which was *The Triumph of England under the Regency,* standing where the castle had once been. At the same time a balloon rose into the air, piloted by one Windham Sadler, who threw a large number of programmes down into the crowd.

Between 1775 and 1856 the Chelsea Waterworks Company had a reservoir in the north-east corner of the park. This is thought to have been where Harriet Westbrook (Shelley's pregnant wife, whom he had deserted) met her mysterious death by drowning in 1816.

At the east side of the park in Cleveland Row, and adjacent to Pall Mall, is Bridgewater House, built by Lord Francis Leveson Gower, second son of the 1st Duke of Sutherland and heir to the Bridgewater estates. He originally inherited Cleveland House but due to its dangerous condition it had to be demolished and was replaced by Bridgewater House which was built to the grand Italianate designs of Charles Barry. It was completed in 1854, though part of the house was opened to the public in 1851 as a picture gallery. It was damaged in World War II, but was sympathetically restored in 1948-9 after which it was sold to the Legal and General Assurance Company. It was then let to the British Oxygen Company, and in turn Tube Investments until 1980 when it was offered for sale for £10 million. It became the home of Greek shipping tycoon John Latsis until his death in 2003, and still remains in private hands.

There is, of course, one owner not mentioned above for Bridgewater House is also Grantham House, the London residence of the Crawleys. The exterior can be seen in Downton Abbey episode 4.9 (*The London Season*) when in the late summer of 1923 almost the whole Downton household decamp to the capital for Rose's coming-out ball. The interior shots were done at Basildon Park (page 12). The house would have been ideal for such an occasion since typically such residences were designed for hosting large parties during the season. The rest of the year it would have remained empty save for the full time housekeeper (Mrs Bute), which probably explains why the family on other visits tended to stay with Lady Rosamund in Belgrave Square (page 95).

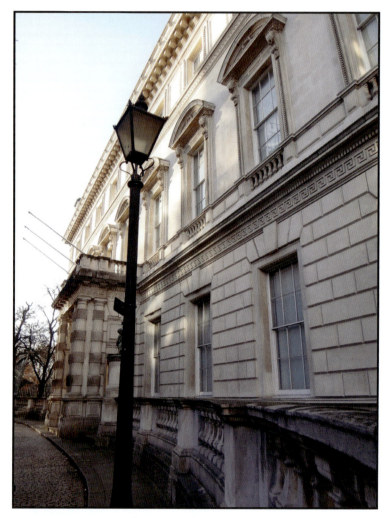

[Bridgewater House, the London residence of the Crawleys]

[Lancaster House is used for government meetings and hospitality]

Almost next door to Bridgewater House is Buckingham Palace, both the real one and the *Downton Abbey* version, Lancaster House whose back garden wall faces The Mall. Again in *The London Season* episode the interior of the building doubles for Buckingham Palace where Lady Rose is presented at court, although some shots where also done at Goldsmiths' Hall in the City of London (page 110), most of the more memorable images of this sequence of the family arriving and ascending the grand staircase and the actual presentation were Lancaster House. Buckingham Palace itself also features in the background for the establishing shots of the family travelling down The Mall en route to the Palace. Originally there were to be more exterior location filming but it clashed with the impending birth of Prince George to the Duchess of Cambridge so many road that were to be used were closed and not accessible for filming.

Originally the site was Godolphin House until 1807 when Frederick, Duke of York, second son of George II, moved here and renamed it York House. Ten years later, following the death of Princess Charlotte, he was heir to the throne and subsequently engaged Robert Smirke to rebuilt York House in a style to reflect the owner's new position. However, the plans were so disliked by the Duke's brother George IV that Smirke was replaced by Benjamin Dean Wyatt. Frederick died before completion, and the estate being in debt was taken over by the government who paid off the debt and

89

subsequently leased the property for £72,000 to the Marquess of Stafford at which time it became Stafford House. In turn he died in 1833 with the house still not finished. The second Duke took on the project asking Wyatt to now plan for the interior decoration and Smirke to carry it out. In 1841 Smirke added another storey for servants.

[The Grand Staircase (top) and Music Room (bottom), both of which doubled as Buckingham Palace when Lady Rose is presented to the King in episode 4.9 of *Downton Abbey*]

The completed mansion was three storeys high with a two storey portico to the front. The exterior was of Bath stone, while the interior was in the French style of Louis XV. The family rooms were all on the ground floor while the spectacular staircase, decorated with imitation marbles and copies of Veronese's paintings, led to the State Drawing Room, the Music Room and the Great Gallery. It was one of the most impressive buildings in London with Queen Victoria often being a guest here and once commenting "I have come from my house to your palace". It was in 1912 after the sale of the house to Sir William Lever that it finally became Lancaster House, and the following year he gave the rest of the lease to the nation so that the house could be used for government hospitality, including the Coronation Banquet for Queen Elizabeth II in 1953. Perhaps most famously the talks which led to the Lancaster House Agreement whereby Zimbabwe obtained an independent constitution were held here in 1979.

Back up in Piccadilly and close to Green Park station is to be found one of the most famous of London establishments, the Ritz Hotel – known simply as The Ritz. It was built for the Blackpool Building and Vendor Company Ltd. on the site of the old Walsingham House and Bath Hotels, to the specific design of Swiss hotelier, César Ritz. He used the same architects as had been employed for the Paris Ritz. The Ritz opened its doors on the 24th May 1906 and at the time was the first major steel-framed building in London. The façade, in a mixture of Portland stone and Norwegian granite, was designed to look like buildings in the Rue de Rivoli in Paris.

The interior is in the style of Louis XVI and has a long gallery with marble floors and crystal chandeliers, a palm court and restaurant with opulent plaster ceilings.

Among the 'Ritzy' people that have visited are Charlie Chaplin who needed forty policemen to clear a path to the door while Pavlova danced within, Noel Coward who wrote here, Talulah Bankhead who famously sipped champagne from her slipper during a press conference, and Churchill, Eisenhower and de Gaulle who met in the Marie Antoinette Suite to confer during World War II. To that list can be added Edith Crawley and her aunt Lady Rosamund who dine in Palm Court and where over dinner Edith is reunited with her ex-fiancé Bertie Pelham revealing his love for her along with a second proposal of marriage. Not only does this scene appear in the last episode of series 6 (*The Christmas Special Finale*), but was, in fact, the very last scene ever filmed with many of the production team dressed in 1920s fashion appearing as background extras.

Earlier in the series (episode 4.4) footman Alfred Nugent who has ambitions to be a chef reads in the newspaper that The Ritz is setting up a training school in honour of Auguste Escoffier the famous French chef with the four winning candidates getting free training and a basic wage plus the chance of a job afterwards. Mrs Patmore thinks that Daisy would be an ideal candidate, but she takes this as a signal that Mrs Patmore wants to get rid of her.

[The Ritz (top) still provides the perfect setting for afternoon tea, while
the Royal Automobile Club (bottom) is splendid for supper]

In the next episode Daisy decides that the best course of action is to help Alfred try to enrol on the training course, albeit that she now dislikes the thought that in doing so she is driving him away from Downton Abbey. Alfred gets his test, which involves him making four dishes including a Vichyssoise but is not one of the four selected. However, as fate would have it Alfred's ambition does come to pass when he receives a letter in which he learns that one of the successful candidates has dropped out having secured a job with the consequence that Alfred exits *Downton Abbey* in episode 4.6 and heads for London and The Ritz. The kitchen scenes were not filmed here but at the Langdon-Downs Centre at Teddington (page 120). Finally The Ritz is also mentioned in episode 5.3 as being the place where the Countess of Grantham and Simon Bricker have dinner, though the viewer never seen them dine.

A short distance away is Pall Mall where at No. 89 is the Royal Automobile Club, founded in 1897 'for the Protection, Encouragement and Development of Automobilism' and first housed at Whitehall Court, then at 119 Piccadilly. The present building, on the site of the Old War Office, was completed in 1911 and designed by the same architects as The Ritz. It is known to be the least intimate of the gentlemen's clubs of London, and was selected by Burgess and Maclean as a suitable place to have lunch before fleeing the country. There are around 17,000 members who, in addition to the usual amenities, have the use of a bookstall, a post office, Turkish baths and a Grecian-style swimming pool. In episode 6.4 of *Downton Abbey* it is here that Henry Talbot invites Lady Mary to supper in the Great Gallery, with some footage of the lobby also being seen.

HOXTON - HOXTON HALL

The area of Hoxton is first referred to in the Domesday Book as a manor of 'three hides' held by the Canons of St. Paul's and worth 45 shillings. In the 14th century William Fitzstephen described it as being 'fields of pasture, and open meadows, very pleasant, into which the river waters do flow, and mills are turned about with a delightful noise'. By the 16th century with the expansion of London the wealthy and fashionable started to move into the surrounding villages with Hoxton becoming a place of entertainment and recreation. The 17th and 18th centuries saw a steady growth in population though Hoxton still retained its rural appearance. It was at this time that many of the city livery companies bought land here and established almshouses. By 1801 Hoxton was part of the Metropolitan Borough of Shoreditch and had a population of nearly 35,000, which by 1861 had grown to around 130,000. As the 20th century dawned the area was said to be 'one of the worst parts of London, where poverty and overcrowding are characteristic of practically the whole district'.

[Hoxton Hall stood in perfectly for the Jubilee Dance Hall in York]

However, Hoxton was still renowned for its entertainment at venues such as the Britannia Theatre, MacDonald's Music Hall, the Varieties and Pollock's Toy Theatre shop. Today the area comprises large council estates interspersed with fashionably reclaimed housing along with a lot of warehouse and workshop conversions. The advent of the Overground railway upgrade has made it an ideal location for city workers. MacDonald's Music Hall, dating from 1863, still exists as Hoxton Hall and is now officially a community centre and performance space to be found at 130 Hoxton Street. The Grade II-listed building is an unrestored example of a saloon-style galleried auditorium. The old music hall lost its license in 1871 and had subsequently been used as a Quaker meeting house, but was restored to its former glory in 2015.

In *Downton Abbey* it appears as the Jubilee Dance Hall, supposedly in York, where in episode 4.2 Lady Rose, chaperoned by Anna Bates, goes in search of some excitement. Lady Rose is soon approached by a local going by the name of Sam Thawley who asks her to dance, and she in turn tells him her name is Rose Smith. While dancing Sam remarks on Lady Rose's posh accent from which he deduces that she must be in service. Lady Rose admits that she lives at Downton Abbey, but implies that she is aspiring to be a lady's maid, and has been working on her accent. The game is nearly up when Jimmy Kent the footman arrives and calls her Lady Rose. However, much worse is to follow when a rival tries to cut in and dance with Lady Rose. This results in a fight on the dance floor. Luckily Jimmy and Anna have the good sense to whisk her off just before the police arrive. Later in the same episode Sam turns up at Downton Abbey hoping to see Rose, who soon appears at the servant's entrance dressed in a maid's uniform. She lets him down gently by saying that she is already promised to a farmer, before kissing him goodbye and wishing him good luck.

HYDE PARK CORNER - BELGRAVE SQUARE

Located at the south-eastern corner of Hyde Park is Hyde Park Corner, which, in essence, is a large roundabout with Apsley House, the home of the first Duke of Wellington at the north side of the junction. In the centre stands the Wellington Arch designed by Decimus Burton and planned as a northern gate to the grounds of Buckingham Palace. On the west side was St. George's Hospital, now the luxury Lanesborough Hotel.

[Belgrave Square under construction in 1827 with Lady Rosamund's residence being the one with a portico closest to the corner]

A few hundred metres to the south is Belgrave Square which takes its name from a Cheshire village. It was in 1826 that the then Earl of Grosvenor obtained planning permission for the area, employing Thomas Cubitt as builder and George Basevi as architect. Bricks for the site were made from the damp clay found in situ, while the excavations were filled with soil from St. Katherine's Dock, also under construction at the time.

[Lady Rosamund's home in Belgrave Square taken from the camera angle most often used so as not to intrude on the privacy of nearby embassies, of which there are many]

The resulting houses were all large stuccoed affairs with no more than a dozen along each side of the square. One time residents have included Lord Sefton (No. 37), Lord Brownlow (No. 12), the Duke of Bedford (No. 15), the Earl of Essex (No. 9), Queen Victoria's mother, the Duchess of Kent (No. 36), Earl Grey (No. 30), the Earl of Eglintoun (No. 10) and the Earl of Pembroke (No. 6) to name but a few. Today the square is mostly embassies with the Syrian Arab (No. 8), Portuguese (No. 11), Austrian (No. 18), Brunei (No. 19), German (No. 23), Norwegian (No. 25), Serbia-Montenegro (No. 28) and Turkish (No. 43) as well as three High Commissions all being located within this ten-acre site. In addition the square is also home to several associations such as the Royal College of Psychiatrists, the Royal College of Defence Studies and the Science & Chemical Industry Society.

To the illustrious names that have inhabited the square must be added that of Lady Rosamund Painswick, widow of the late Duke Marmaduke, who resides at No. 35. This is only half true for although the exterior shots in *Downton Abbey* are of Belgrave Square, all the interior scenes were done at West Wycombe Park (page 29). Her house is obviously very comfortable since when visiting London for a few days the Crawleys invariably seem to stay here, rather than at their own residence, Grantham House (page 87).

[The landing by the Argyll Room featured as the Embassy Club in
***The London Season* episode of *Downton Abbey*]**

On the southern boundary of Hyde Park, and close to Hyde Park Corner, is Hamilton Place, which was originally a cul-de-sac leading out of Piccadilly. It is named after James Hamilton, who was appointed Ranger to the park by his companion King Charles II. No. 4 was once the home of the Earl of Lucan (1810), the Duke of Wellington (1814) and Lord Granville

(1822). Today is the headquarters of the Royal Aeronautical Society. The current building dates from 1906 and is decorated in the Louis XVI style most associated with The Ritz (page 91). No. 4 Hamilton Place is also an exclusive conference and wedding venue.

[The splendid baroque staircase that Lady Rose and Madeleine Allsopp climb at the Embassy Club]

It is here in *Downton Abbey* episode 4.9 (*The London Season*) that Lady Rose MacClare and Madeleine Allsopp ascend the baroque staircase to the Argyll Room, which doubles as the Embassy Club, and are introduced to the Prince of Wales who just happens to be seated at a table with Madeleine's father. The room also became the restaurant of The Netherby, the posh hotel close to Downton, where Mr. Bates and Anna go for a romantic evening. The snobbish *maître d'hotel* cannot find a reservation and refuses them entry
until they say that they know the Countess of Grantham who, it transpires, is also dining there that evening. The countess comes over to say hello to them, with the result that a table suddenly becomes available.

KING'S CROSS - ST. PANCRAS STATION

[The Gothic exterior and eastern clock tower of St. Pancras
station, with Britannia, on top of the gable to the right
of the tower, looking down on King's Cross station]

King's Cross, an area straddling the boroughs of Camden and Islington,
was known for much of its modern existence as a red light district. A lot
has changed, though, over the past decade, in large part thanks to the new
British Library building and the adjacent St. Pancras International railway
station, which is now the London terminus of Eurostar services to the
Continent. Indeed, some £500 million has been spend on the regeneration
of this area since 2005.

99

Battle Bridge was the original name, since it was where a bridge once crossed the River Fleet. However, there is no evidence of any battle at this site, though unsupported folk lore has it that this was the scene of a major conflict between the Romans and Iceni tribe led by Boudica, and it is even suggested that Boudica was killed and is buried here, at what is now the area between platforms 9 and 10 at King's Cross station (maybe the inspiration for platform $9^3/4$ of the Harry Potter books) and where her ghost is sometimes reported to manifest itself. Even if this is not true, the station is certainly built on the site of a former smallpox hospital.

The current name is derived from 1830, when a monument to King George IV was built at the junction of Gray's Inn Road, Pentonville Road, and New Road (which later became Euston Road, and marked the outer boundary of London). The monument was eighteen metres high and topped by a three metre tall statue of the King. It was not popular, being described as 'a ridiculous octagonal structure crowned by an absurd statue', and was demolished in 1845. The upper part was used as a *camera obscura*, while the base in turn housed a police station and a public house. The site is now occupied by King's Cross station, one of the so called 'railway cathedrals', designed by Lewis Cubitt and opened in 1852.

Meanwhile St. Pancras railway station, built on the site of the old Agar Town slums, is a far more splendid structure. The name is that of a fourteen-year-old boy who converted to Christianity and was martyred by the Emperor Diocletian.

The station, was built between 1863-7, is a single shed, some two hundred and ten metres long by seventy-three metres wide and thirty metres high at its apex. It was constructed of glass and iron to the design of W. H. Barlow, and at the time was the largest single span structure of its type in the world. The station is set higher than its neighbour by some six metres due to the Regent's Canal, but the space beneath the station was not wasted, since it was always intended to be used for the storage of beer barrels from Burton-on-Trent, the iron supporting columns being spaced in measurements of beer barrels so as to maximise the available area.

Unlike King's Cross station, which has a plain front and a hotel to the side, St. Pancras station built its Midland Grand Hotel right on Euston Road. As it was to be a symbol for the importance of the Midland Railway no expense was spared. In fact, of the eleven designs submitted by various architects in 1865, that which was accepted by the company was the most expensive plan at £316,000 (though the final bill was £438,000). This was the design by George Gilbert Scott, who envisaged a high Gothic style construction consisting of pinnacles, towers and gables and, in contrast to

King's Cross station, was said by the architect himself to be 'possibly too good for its purpose'. It has been said by others to be 'the finest building in London'. The structure is one hundred and seventy-two metres long, with a west tower seventy-six metres high and an east clock tower even higher at eighty-two metres. Standing on a gable beside the east tower is a bronze statue of Britannia (actually part of the lightning conductor) who is said the have her back to Euston station while looking down on King's Cross station. The hotel had two hundred and fifty bedrooms and was said to be 'the most sumptuous and best-conducted hotel in the empire'.

[The spot where Edith is picked up by Burns the chauffeur]

The hotel was ahead of its time in many respects – it was the first building in London to have a revolving door installed, and guests could listen in to theatre and concert performances through the hotel's telephone system – but it lacked other amenities, such as central heating and *en suite* bathrooms, which by the 20th century most guests considered essential. Patronage declined, and in 1935 it closed and became railway offices, changing its name to St. Pancras Chambers. The building also suffered because Scott used Edward Gripper's patent bricks, which were dressed with several different types of stone (such as red and grey Peterhead granite) which, although magnificent in looks, are porous and so weather far more quickly than the ordinary London bricks of King's Cross station. With the ever-mounting expense of upkeep, the whole building was left to slowly become a relic of a past era – sad and unsafe to enter. There were frequent calls for demolition, but when St. Pancras was announced as the new terminus for Eurostar trains a saviour was at hand. From 2003 to 2007 the whole area was redeveloped, with a large new building to the north for suburban services and the opening up of the vaults to house the new booking hall and shopping area. The former hotel has been refurbished to become once again a first class hotel with private apartments.

Films shot here include *The Ipcress File* (1965), *Brannigan* (1975), *Voyage of the Damned* (1976), *McVicar* (1980), *The Fourth Protocol* (1987), *Shirley Valentine* (1989), *King Ralph* (1991), *Shining Through* (1992), *Chaplin* (1992), *Howards End* (1992), *The Secret Garden* (1993), *102 Dalmatians* (2000), *Batman Begins* (2005), *Somers Town* (2008), *Harry Potter and the Chamber of Secrets* (2002) and *Harry Potter and the Deathly Hallows: Part 2* (2011).

In episode 4.1 it to St. Pancras that Edith arrives by train from Downton and is met by Michael Gregson who wishes to suggest the idea of them living in Germany in order for him to get a divorce from his wife on grounds of lunacy. They are seen walking out under the arch to be greeted by Burns, the chauffeur who Lady Rosamund has sent to collect her. The scene is a little wrong since trains from Yorkshire would arrive at the adjacent King's Cross, though the actual train Edith gets off at St. Pancras is itself a little lost having started its journey on the Bluebell Railway in Sussex (page 188). For filming this shot a large black hoarding with a smoke generator behind was put in place to cover up the Eurostar trains just behind.

NOTTING HILL GATE - CHEPSTOW VILLAS

It was only in the 1840s when demand for housing began to rise that the whole area, which up until then had been solely agricultural, was developed. Much of the land belonged to the Ladbroke estate and was sold off in parcels by the family to speculators, though James Weller Ladbroke did retain the eastern part of what is now Chepstow Villas. The central part of the road was bought by Robert Hall of Old Bond Street, and later in 1847 following the death of James Ladbroke his heir Felix Ladbroke sold the western plot to the Reverend Brooke Edward Bridges from

Bedfordshire, who in turn sold it on to Thomas Pocock. The landowners signed 99-year lease agreements with a number of professional builders as well as individuals who were interested in property speculation. This explains the variety of styles in this single street. One of the main developers was William Henry Jenkins who hailed from Herefordshire on the Welsh borders, and it is he who decided the names for the new streets, choosing the names of places near his home – Chepstow, Denbigh, Ledbury and Pembridge.

[A typical house in Chepstow Villas illustrates why it is such a sought after street in the Royal Borough of Kensington and Chelsea]

The houses were inhabited, in the main, by professional people such as solicitors, schoolteachers, civil engineers, surgeons, stockbrokers and merchants, with each property having several servants. However, by the 20th century many of the properties had been divided into flats and the neighbourhood was described by novelist Monica Dickens as being 'like

Clapham right on the edge of the slums'. Today the area has undergone regeneration and gentrification and is again a sought after location.

[The Shaw studio which became Lady Edith's London flat]

As far as *Downton Abbey* is concerned it is No. 42/42a that is of interest. The main house was a low-built detached villa and home to the Victorian animal painter Thomas Sidney Cooper. In about 1875 he commissioned Richard Norman Shaw to build the studio (No. 42a) that stands in the garden around the corner in Denbigh Road. It is this studio that became Edith's London flat that she inherited from Michael Gregson. It first appears in episode 4.1, though as the series continues it became more expedient to build a set for it back at Ealing Studios.

PICCADILLY CIRCUS - CRITERION RESTAURANT

Piccadilly Circus was formed in 1819 at the intersection with John Nash's new Regent Street. Later, in the mid-1880s, what was an elegant and symmetric crossroads was destroyed when Shaftesbury Avenue, along with the London Pavilion, was built, making it into something resembling a vortex. The harmony of the area was further destroyed with the erection of electrically illuminated advertisements, and despite objections to the London County Council, who were sympathetic, nothing was done, and so by 1910 the area had large electric signs advertising both Bovril and Schweppes. In 1923 the London Pavilion was also covered, even though the owner was the London County Council itself, who no doubt found consolation in the lucrative rents achieved from the advertisements. Other parts of Piccadilly Circus are Crown property, and here the leasing agreements do not permit any such advertising. In the 1980s and 1990s many of the buildings were refurbished, including the London Pavilion (which is currently free of any such electronic signs).

In the refurbishment the road layout was changed and the area around Eros (actually the Shaftesbury Memorial Fountain) made a pedestrian zone. The monument, the first statue to be constructed entirely of aluminium, was designed by Alfred Gilbert and was erected by public donations in memory of the 7th Earl of Shaftesbury, a well-known philanthropist. The statue above the fountain was meant to represent the Angel of Christian Charity, and not Eros (the God of Love). In fact the whole structure was not as it was meant to be, since the fountain itself was not to Gilbert's original design, having a much smaller basin to collect the water, with the consequence that if turned on fully it drenches passers-by. Most visitors do not even realise that it is a fountain. So disgusted was Gilbert with the changes made to his plans that he refused to attend the opening ceremony. Today Eros has become such an integral part of London life that on various occasions, such as New Year's Eve, it has been boarded up to keep the public from climbing it, and during World War II it was removed altogether and stored at Egham in Surrey, so that any invading army could not make propaganda from its capture or destruction.

Although above ground there is no circus (circular structure), underneath there is an almost perfect circular booking hall for the Underground station, which was designed by Charles Holden and S. A. Heaps in 1925-8. This was the first Underground station to be built entirely underground with access only by subways from street level.

As it is in the very centre of London and so recognisable to film audiences around the world, it will come as no surprise to learn that this area has appeared on the silver screen in around sixty major productions. Among the most memorable are *An American Werewolf in London* (1981) in which David Naughton turns into a werewolf inside the Eros cinema and subsequently causes carnage outside in Piccadilly Circus itself, *Brannigan* (1975) in which John Wayne waits for the ransom money to be collected from a fake post box here, *Bridget Jones's Diary* (2001) where Bridget's daily consumption is displayed on the advertising display behind her as she walks past, *Bridget Jones: The Edge of Reason* (2004) when the display this time more happily proclaims that Bridget and Mark are the real thing and *The Dark Knight* (2008) in which Christian Bale as Bruce Wayne eats at the Criterion restaurant at Piccadilly Circus.

[The Criterion Restaurant at Piccadilly Circus]

Another visitor to this restaurant was Lady Edith who sees Michael Gregson here in *Downton Abbey* episode 4.1. She arrives by car to the front of the restaurant, which is actually a pedestrian area, and then immediately afterwards appears at the back of the building making her way down the steps towards the front to meet Michael. They sit in the Long Bar with its ceiling of gold mosaics and over drinks he tells her that he is willing to become a German citizen just so he can get a divorce and marry her. The scene ends with a kiss.

[The Long Bar with gold mosaic ceiling and other decoration]

It also appears in episode 6.6 as the place where Lady Mary and Tom Branson dine in the upper part of the restaurant as members of the "... party of singletons" as the former puts it. Lady Mary sits next to Henry Talbot who mentions that he will be racing at Brooklands soon, and invites her and Tom along to watch. This encounter also ends in a kiss, but this time it is not in the restaurant, but on their walk afterwards through the deserted streets of London (actually filmed in Middle Temple Lane, page 128).

The Criterion Restaurant was built at a cost of £80,000 between 1870 and 1874 by Thomas Verity for Spiers and Pond, the railway caterers, on the site of the old White Bear Inn. The concert hall in the basement became the Criterion Theatre. The restaurant was one of the earliest buildings to use ornamental tiles for decoration along with semi-precious stones such as jade, mother of pearl and turquoise to complete the Neo-Byzantine style. Luckily its Grade I listed interior was left intact when it was taken over by celebrity chef Marco Pierre White in 1995. Since then it has changed hands, and following a brief period of closure is now operated by Savini. There is a plaque in the Long Bar commemorating the fact that it was here in *A Study in Scarlet* that one Dr. John H. Watson talks with Stamford, his dresser at Barts and learns of his prospective roommate – Sherlock Holmes.

Finally there is a shot of Anna pausing beside Eros after delivering a note to Lord Gillingham at the request of Lady Mary in episode 5.4, while it was in Piccadilly that Mr. Green was killed in episode 4.8.

St. James's Park - St. James's Park

The park takes its name from the hospital for leper women, on the site where St. James's Palace now stands. It is the oldest of the London royal parks, extending to around 90 acres and bounded by The Mall to the north and Birdcage Walk to the south. At the western end are the Queen Victoria Memorial and Buckingham Palace, while Horse Guards Road forms the eastern perimeter. The site has had different uses over the years. King Henry VIII had a bowling alley erected, and Queen Elizabeth I hunted here. It was King James I who had the space first laid out with formal gardens, along with a menagerie (which included two crocodiles), a physic garden and an aviary.

After the execution of King Charles I the park was neglected and most of the trees were felled for fuel. It was left to King Charles II to extend the park and lay it out afresh, which included converting several of the smaller ponds into one strip of water known as the Canal. By the reign of Queen Anne the place was notorious for prostitution, and the *New Critical Review* complained of the 'stagnant water in the lake and the trees and scrubs all wanting attention'. With the appointment of Lord Pomfret as Ranger in 1751 things began to improve. From as early as 1623, cows were grazed in the park, and a French visitor in 1765 reported that 'the cows are driven about noon and evening to the gate which leads from the Park to the quarter of Whitehall. Tied in a file to posts at the extremity of the grass plot, they will swill passengers with their milk, which being drawn from their udders on the spot is served with all cleanliness peculiar to the English, in little mugs at the rate of 1d per mug.'

[View from the park looking toward Buckingham Palace. It is along the path just to the left of this picture that Lady Mary and Lady Rosamund walk and talk]

In an effort to curb the prostitution the gates to the park were locked at night, but this had little affect since there were some six and a half thousand authorised key holders, plus thousands of others who had obtained keys unofficially. The park was also known for duelling, though it was never as popular here as in other London parks, and to draw a sword within its boundaries was illegal.

In 1814 a lavish gala was held to celebrate the anniversaries of the Battle of the Nile and the accession to the English throne of the House of Hanover. A seven-storey Chinese pagoda was built, along with a picturesque yellow bridge, ornamented with black lines and a bright blue roof, that spanned the canal. The bridge remained in place until 1825, though the pagoda did not last as long: it caught fire during the celebration fireworks, killing the lamplighter and injuring five other workmen.

Further improvements to the park were made after King George IV came to the throne. Gas lighting was installed in 1822, and four years later the Canal was remodelled into the graceful curved lake that we see today. (It may look natural, but in 1855 the lake was dredged and concrete lined to a uniform depth of four feet.) Trees were planted and new walkways laid out.

In episode 1.7 of *Downton Abbey* Lady Mary and her aunt Lady Rosamund walk along the southern path beside the lake, with Buckingham Palace in the background. Lady Rosamund is eager to know if Lady Mary has made a decision about marrying cousin Matthew, or whether she is keeping anything from her. There is also a wonderful observation about the English weather: to Rosamund's comment, "There's nothing like an English summer, is there?" her niece replies, "Except an English winter." Rosamund herself makes an insightful remark when, after noting that Lady Mary has not received many social invitations, she adds, "After four seasons one is less a debutant than a survivor." In the same episode, and shot at the same time, is the scene showing Anna, walking through the park (in the wrong direction) on her way to Bates's former barracks (actually the Royal Chelsea Hospital) in order to ascertain whether he was guilty of stealing the regimental silver. It is also where in episode 5.9 Atticus Aldridge and Lady Rose are seen arguing over the compromising photographs taken during his stag party.

ST. PAUL'S - GOLDSMITHS' HALL

This area within the City of London is most famous, of course, for the cathedral, the one standing today being the fourth to occupy the site. The Wren masterpiece rather dominates the area, but there are other fine buildings to be found here. One of these is Goldsmiths' Hall located in Foster Lane. The first record of a hall dates from 1366 when it was the residence of Nicholas de Seagrave, brother of the then Bishop of London. Over the next three centuries various additions were made, including in the courtyard, an assay office, vaults, an armoury and a granary.

The next hall was built by Nicholas Stone in 1634 and was used as the exchequer by the Parliamentarians during the Civil War and up to 1660. Unfortunately this building was damaged in the Great Fire of 1666, but restored in 1669. The present structure is in the Renaissance-style and was built on the same site between 1829 and 1835. It was again subject to damage in World War II but restored in 1947. The panelling in the main Court Room is from the 1669 hall.

The Goldsmiths' Company is ranked the 5th among City Livery Companies and received its first charter in 1327. In 1300 gold and silver were first marked with a leopard's head by the wardens of the craft, which soon became one of the most wealthy and powerful of the so called 'great companies'. It had absolute responsibility for the quality of gold and silver (and now platinum) objects, which after 1478 had to have the Goldsmiths' hallmark. The Company still operates the London Assay Office on site.

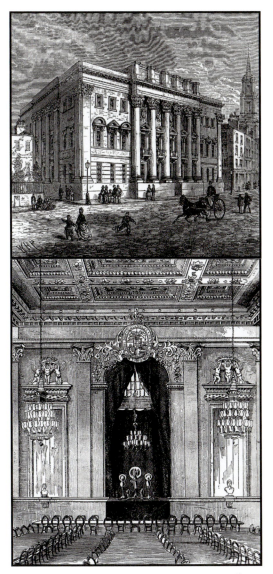

[The exterior (top) and Livery Hall (bottom) from 19th century prints]

[Marble statues by Samuel Nixon representing the Four Seasons, and the bust of King William IV in the Staircase Hall]

The Hall can be seen in *Daniel Deronda* (2002), *The Lost Prince* (2003), *Woman in Gold* (2015), *The Legend of Tarzan* (2016) and most recently in the Netflix series *The Crown* (2016). It also doubles for some of the interiors of Buckingham Palace in episode 4.9, *The London Season*, of *Downton Abbey*, though most of the key scenes in that sequence were shot at Lancaster House (page 89).

SLOANE SQUARE - ROYAL HOSPITAL CHELSEA

Sloane Square is named after Sir Hans Sloane who was at one time lord of the Manor of Chelsea. In 1771 the grassland was enclosed and cobbled, with houses being built around the square some years later. The Underground railway station was opened in 1868, but not without some difficulty since the River Westbourne runs across the station, and still does today, being carried over the tracks in a large iron pipe. The station suffered a direct hit from a bomb during World War II, with many casualties from the two trains that happened to be standing in the station at the time. The station restoration took eleven years to complete, re-opening in 1951 in time for the Festival of Britain. The two most prominent buildings around the square are Peter Jones, a department store originally opened by a young Welsh draper's assistant in 1877, and the Royal Court Theatre. In the centre of the square is a fountain, by the sculptor Gilbert Ledward, which was unveiled in 1951. It consists of a kneeling bronze figure of Venus, holding a vase and pouring water from a conch shell. The basin is decorated with a relief depicting Charles II and Nell Gwynn seated by the River Thames.

To the south of Sloane Square is the Royal Hospital Chelsea, founded by King Charles II as a residence for British soldiers who are unfit for further duty due to injury or old age. The inspiration came from the Hôtel des Invalides in Paris. The hospital is set in spacious and beautiful grounds beside Royal Hospital Road.

[Figure Court where Anna waits to the right of the portico for information on Bates]

The site chosen was that of an unsuccessful College of Theology, established in 1618 by Dr. Sutcliffe, Dean of Exeter. After only forty years the college closed, and the premises were taken over by the government to house Dutch and Scottish prisoners of war. In 1666, after the Great Fire, the building was offered to the Royal Society, but it had become so dilapidated that the Society rejected it in favour of Arundel House. Fifteen years later, Sir Stephen Fox, the first Paymaster General, outlined the idea of a military hostel to King Charles II, and the following year Christopher Wren was appointed architect with the King laying the foundation stone. In fact the King was only able to contribute around £7,000, and a public

113

subscription raised little more. The real hero, without whom the hospital would never have been built, was Fox himself, who surrendered his commission as Paymaster General and donated £13,000 to the establishing of the Royal Hospital. Such deductions from army pay and pensions provided the main funding for the hospital until 1847, when Parliament stepped in and ensured financial security for the hospital thereafter.

The hospital is built around three courtyards. Figure Court, named after the bronzed statue of Charles II, designed by Grinling Gibbons, which dominates the centre, looks southwards, towards the River Thames. It is flanked by Light Horse Court and College Court, opening to the east and west respectively. Light Horse Court (which takes its name from the Light Horse Guards, who until 1850 were ranked below the Horse Guards but above the infantry) is actually a replica of the original Wren building, which was heavily damaged by enemy bombing in 1918 and destroyed by a V2 rocket in 1945. College Court is home to the Orderly and Master Butler rooms (not open to the public), the interiors of which doubled as wards in Downton cottage hospital.

[College Court with the Master Butler room to the right]

Figure Court is the oldest, and architecturally most impressive, part of the hospital. Along the northern range are the Chapel and Great Hall, linked by an octagonal vestibule. The cornice above the colonnade that runs the entire length of the range bears a Latin inscription to the effect that the Hospital is for the support and relief of maimed and superannuated soldiers, and that it was founded by Charles II, enlarged by James II and completed by William and Mary in 1692. In episode 1.7 of *Downton Abbey* we see Anna walking past the statue of King Charles II and to the colonnade, to enquire after Bates's army record. The Royal Hospital doubles perfectly for the Duke of York regimental barracks where Bates is supposed to have served. Anna should really have looked exhausted, though, for in the preceding scene we saw her walking through St. James's Park some two miles away (page 108). The sergeant she meets asks her to wait, and she obliges by sitting next to the entrance to the vestibule. Her patience is rewarded when the sergeant returns with the address of Bates's mother, whom she later visits.

When the Duke of Wellington's body lay in state in the Great Hall, so many people came to see his coffin that two were killed in the crush. In the Chapel, a rare example of Wren's pure ecclesiastical work, besides the painting of the Resurrection and the fine woodwork, one should note the magnificent silver-gift altar plate made by Ralph Leete and hallmarked 1687-8. At the southern end of the east wing is the Governor's House, whose State Room boasts fine limewood carvings. Royal portraits by the likes of Van Dyck, Lely and Kneller line the walls. Also on the eastern side is the Margaret Thatcher Infirmary, opened by the Prince of Wales in 2009. The original infirmary, designed by Sir John Soane, was at the other end of the hospital, but it was destroyed by a landmine in 1941. The main buildings have remained virtually unchanged in design, although there were some minor alterations by Robert Adam in 1765-82, and stables were added by Sir John Soane in 1814. Thomas Carlyle observed that the hospital was 'quiet and dignified and the work of a gentleman'.

The hospital is generally open to the public on weekdays and Sunday afternoons. Visitors may walk around the public areas and visit the small museum which outlines the hospital's history. The museum is entered via Wellington Hall, which contains a variety of objects associated with the great Duke, including two captured French 'eagles' and the gigantic painting depicting the Battle of Waterloo by George Jones. Best of all, visitors are encouraged to engage with the In-Pensioners, who are always on hand, and easily spotted in their magnificent scarlet coats and ceremonial tricorn hats, and ready to tell a story or two. Prospective visitors should check www.chelsea-pensioners.org.uk. Finally, each May the Chelsea Flower Show is held in the grounds, attracting many thousands of visitors every day.

115

SOUTH KENSINGTON - HYDE PARK

[The Albert Memorial, a great place for a picnic]

Just over 2 miles from Charing Cross is the affluent district of South Kensington known for its museums in Exhibition Road, the Royal Albert Hall, Imperial College London, the Royal College of Arts, the Royal College of Music and Baden-Powell House. Along the northern boundary is the largest of the Royal Parks – Hyde Park. After the Norman Conquest it was a place of deer, boars and wild bulls having been bequeathed to the monks of Westminster. On the Dissolution of the Monasteries in 1536 it became the property of King Henry VIII who hunted here. It was not opened to the public until the 17th century, though during the Civil War it became an area of military camps and fortifications for the Parliamentarians. It was sold for £17,000 in 1652 after which it became a place for the wealthy to parade and be seen. King Charles II took the park back into royal hands in 1660, and had it enclosed with a brick wall. It now became notorious for highwaymen, and even the Prime Minister Horace Walpole was attacked here in 1749, losing eight guineas to two men armed with a blunderbuss. It was also famous as a duelling ground.

It is Queen Caroline who was responsible for having the lake known as the Serpentine being formed by damming the River Westbourne in 1730. This effectively divided the park in two with the western part becoming known as Kensington Gardens. The park is most famous for the Great Exhibition of 1851, which was held in the Crystal Palace built exclusively for the event. Interestingly, it was not until 1860 that flowers were first planted in the park by the landscape gardener William Nesfield who was also responsible for the Italian Water Garden. It was during the Victorian period that the park was adorned with statues, fountains and the other buildings that are still here today.

Two of the most visited are the Albert Memorial and Peter Pan's Statue. The former is on the south side of the park in Kensington Gardens right opposite the Royal Albert Hall. It was unveiled in 1872 and was the work of George Gilbert Scott, who designed it to commemorate the death of Prince Albert. The memorial shows Prince Albert holding the catalogue of the Great Exhibition, which he inspired and helped organise. There are marble figures representing Europe, Asia, Africa and America at each corner, and higher up there are figures representing manufacture, commerce, agriculture and engineering, while near the top are gilded bronze statues of the angles and virtues. Around the base is a Parnassus frieze depicting celebrated painters, poets, musicians and the like – 187 carved figures in all. Without doubt it is one of the grandest high-Victorian gothic extravaganzas anywhere in the world.

There is no mistaking it when it appears in the *Downton Abbey* episode 4.9, *The London Season*, when Harold Levinson, Madeleine Allsopp, William Allsopp, Martha Levinson and Violet have a picnic here that has been prepared by Daisy Mason and is served by Ethan Slade (Harold's American valet). When Slade informs Mrs. Hughes that they are meeting at "A place called the Albert memorial, but ah, will I know it when I see it?" she replies, "You most certainly will, I can promise you that." Most of the filming for this scene was not done in Hyde Park at all, but in the grounds of Basildon Park (page 12). Later in episode 5.4 the park features again, but this time it is Peter Pan's statue that makes a rather poignant appearance.

The park is the setting for J. M. Barrie's book *Peter Pan in Kensington Gardens*, a prelude to the character's appearance in *Neverland*. It was J. M. Barrie himself who commissioned Sir George Frampton to build the statue in 1902, though it was not installed in Kensington Gardens until 1912. The statue features squirrels, rabbits, mice and fairies climbing up to Peter Pan. Its location is significant for it is in the exact spot where Peter Pan lands having flown out of the nursery in *The Little White Bird*.

**[The Peter Pan statue beside the
Long water in Kensington Gardens]**

This time it is Lady Mary and Lord Gillingham who are seen in the park. It is beside the statue at midday – which is more appropriate for bad news as Lady Mary puts it – that she informs him that her feelings have changed, though as she says to Charles Blake the night before at dinner she is "… very fond of him", and "…will always be fond of him". Charles can only think that the spot chosen is inappropriate commenting, "Crumbs, wont the setting make him dream of happy families?" Lord Gillingham, as predicted, does not take it well, and beyond that refuses to give in stating that "… we will get through this together".

SYON LANE - SYON HOUSE

The area takes its name from the monastery of the Bridgettine Order founded in 1415 by King Henry V, which stood until the 16th century on the north bank of the River Thames, close to Isleworth in west London. In turn the monastery took its name from the Biblical Holy 'City of David which is Zion'.

[The Great Conservatory, designed by Charles Fowler, where Lord Gillingham and Lady Mary lunch]

After the Dissolution of the Monasteries it was used as a place of confinement for Catherine Howard prior to her execution in 1542. Later in 1547 King Henry VIII's coffin rested here on its way from Westminster to Windsor. During the night it burst open and the following morning dogs were discovered licking up certain remains.

The house seen today dates from the time of King Edward VI when Edward Seymour, Duke of Somerset, Protector of the Realm, acquired the estate from the Crown. However, he was executed in 1552 for felony with the estate passing to John Dudley, Duke of Northumberland, and it was here that his daughter-in-law Lady Jane Grey was offered the Crown. Dudley was also executed with the estate once again reverting to the

119

monarch. In 1594 Queen Elizabeth I granted a lease to Henry Percy, 9th Earl of Northumberland – the house remains in the family to this day, and has since 1995, during the time of the 12th Duke, been open to the public.

The main house is a stone-built turreted quadrangle with various additions having been made over the centuries. The 10th Earl had Inigo Jones make repairs and improvements, while the 1st Duke had Robert Adam improve the house during which time Lancelot 'Capability' Brown landscaped the grounds. It was Adam that was responsible for creating a magnificent suite of rooms which includes the great hall, the ante-room which is lavishly gilded and adorned in the Roam style, the dining room with its richly ornamented half-domes screened by columns at each end, the red drawing room with its crimson silk walls, and the long gallery which has unusual proportions of 41.5 metres long and only 4.3 metres wide and high.

Of particular note for the *Downton Abbey* enthusiast is the Great Conservatory, which was designed by Charles Fowler and constructed from gunmetal and Bath stone. It is said that it was the inspiration for Joseph Paxton who studied it before designing Crystal Palace. In episode 4.8 it becomes the restaurant at which Lord Gillingham and Lady Mary have lunch in London, and where she asks him to have Mr. Green dismissed without any questions being asked.

TEDDINGTON - NORMANSFIELD THEATRE

Teddington, located in the London Borough of Richmond, just over 10 miles south-west of Charing Cross, was formerly in the county of Middlesex. The area is mainly residential, interspersed with shops and offices. There is no industry here as such, but it is the home to Teddington Studios (former base of Thames Television and now part of the Pinewood Studios Group), and the National Physical Laboratory. Also at Teddington was a remarkable hospital, Normansfield, dedicated to the care of those with learning difficulties.

The founder was Dr. John Haydon Langdon-Down, who gave his name to the condition known as Down's Syndrome. He was born in Cornwall in 1828, and, after qualifying at the London Hospital in 1858, accepted the post of Superintendent of the Asylum for Idiots at Earlswood, the first institution of its kind in the country. Having gained a working experience of such matters, he then acquired a recently built house on the Kingston Road, named Normansfield, which he opened as a private nursing home in

1868. It was for the 'care, education and treatment of those of good social position who present a degree of mental deficiency'. Over the next twenty years the number of patients increased from the initial twenty to one hundred and fifty. As a consequence extensions were built. The hospital also farmed 40 acres of land, where there were cows, chickens and a herd of black and middle white pigs, as well as a productive garden, which provided food for the kitchens, making the community self-sufficient in many respects. Activities for the patients included dancing, gymnastics, music, languages, driving, riding, all manner of sports, boating, entertainments and seaside visits.

[The scene of high drama at the annual Downton flower show as Mr. Molesley's roses beat the display by the Dowager Countess]

When Langdon-Down died in 1896 his wife took over, and on her death in 1901 the responsibility passed to their two sons, Reginald and Percival, who ensured that modern advances in medical knowledge and occupation therapy were reflected in the life at the hospital. In 1951 the hospital became part of the NHS, but Reginald remained at the helm, and after his death Percival's son Norman took over as Physician Superintendent. In 1957 a League of Friends of Normansfield was formed, one of its most active fundraisers being the actor-manager Brian Rix.

The connection with the name of Langdon-Down was only severed in 1970 upon the retirement of Norman. By 1974, Normansfield was recognised as a 'problem hospital', run by a psychiatrist who was described as 'arrogant' and 'incompetent'. In May 1976 most of the nurses went on strike, and the senior manager was suspended. An official investigation found fault with most of the management of the Hospital. Several nursing officers and administrators were dismissed, including the senior manager. The hospital was closed in 1997, and has been redeveloped as a housing estate.

What remains, however, is the beautiful Grade II* listed theatre wing of the former hospital, now owned and managed by the Down's Syndrome Association. It was built in 1877 as the entertainment hall and is a rare example of a private Victorian Theatre, complete with original painted scenery and other ornate fixtures and fittings. In fact it is one of only two theatres remaining that has the original Victorian side flaps in working order. Built to the design of Rowland Plumbe, it was opened in 1879 by the Earl of Devon. At sixty feet by thirty-five feet, with seating for three hundred people, it is remarkably large for a private theatre. The proscenium paintings have no stylistic parallel in any London theatre. Over the doors are four excellent life-size painted figures of Tragedy, Painting, Music and Comedy. The paintings of wild flowers and grasses on the door panels at the front of the stage are thought to be the work of Marianne North. On the theatre walls are six of the twenty-one life-size portraits painted for the 1888 production of *Ruddigore* at the Savoy Theatre. They were framed with central swivels at the top and bottom, allowing actors to step out, bringing the pictures to life.

Today the theatre is still in use for a host of productions, ranging from opera to Music Hall. There are also workshops run for adults and children, covering drama, art and photography. In addition the site houses the Langdon Down Museum of Learning Disability, which is open to the public on Monday afternoons and Saturday mornings. For further information on all aspects of the Langdon Down Centre please visit their web site (www.langdondowncentre.org.uk).

The Normansfield Theatre doubled as Downton Village Hall in episode 1.5 of the series. This is where the annual Downton flower show is held, which by tradition the Dowager Countess has always dominated and won, due to her position in the village. However, this situation changes with the arrival of Isobel Crawley, who is adamant that the winner should be decided on merit rather than status, and repeatedly hints that the roses entered by Bill Molesley are the best exhibit. In the event, when the Dowager Countess opens the envelope to announce the winner she sees that her name, as usual, is written on the piece of paper, but, deciding that Isobel Crawley is correct, reads out the name of Bill Molesley, much to the latter's delight.

The Langdon-Down Centre also doubled for the Ritz kitchens in *Downton Abbey* episode 4.4 when Alfred Nugent takes his exam in order to become a candidate for their new training school.

TEMPLE - LINCOLN'S INN FIELDS & NEW SQUARE/STONE BUILDINGS MIDDLE TEMPLE NO. 2 TEMPLE PLACE

The area known as Temple lies at the heart of London's legal district. It takes its name from the Inner Temple and Middle Temple, two of the four Inns of Court, which occupy land in the City of London once owned by the Knights Templar. On the other side of the road, in the City of Westminster, are the Royal Courts of Justice. From Temple Underground station it is a short walk up Surrey Street to Aldwych and thence to Kingsway on the far side, from which Sardinia Street a little way up on the right leads to Lincoln's Inn Fields. The fields in the name are Purse Field and Cup Field, which had been a playground for students at Lincoln's Inn since the 14th century, but now comprise London's largest square. They both became Crown property in around 1537 after which they were best known as a place of execution – Anthony Babington, Hugh Moore and Robert Morton being among those hanged here. It wasn't until the 1630s that William Newton gained permission to build thirty-two houses on the site, and thus the genesis of the square as it is known today. Although a fashionable place to live it was still blighted by the odd execution as well as numerous fights and robberies that took place in the vicinity. Today some 18th century houses remain, along with Sir John Soane's Museum along the north side of the square.

In *Downton Abbey* series 4 it was the backdrop of period houses that made the square ideal for the location of Lady Rosamund, Lady Edith and Lady Rose's evening strolls.

Adjacent to Lincoln's Inn Fields is a plain square, New Square, set out between 1685 and 1697 on the former Ficket's Field of the Knights Templar by the barrister and speculator Henry Serle. At the southern end is Lincoln's Inn Archway to Carey Street, while at the north is a splendid iron screen, made in 1863, with two stone water pumps in front of it. In *Downton Abbey* episode 6.3 it is by the archway that Lady Edith meets Bertie Pelham and is persuaded to have drinks with him that evening at Rules Restaurant (page 76).

123

[Lincoln's Inn Fields is the ideal spot for an evening stroll (top) while New Square is the place to bump into old acquaintances (bottom)]

In episodes 6.2 the square again appears as the location of *The Sketch* as Lady Edith and Lady Rosamund emerge from No. 7 talking about Marigold and the latest proposals for the Downton cottage hospital.

[Stone Buildings is not an obvious route for London buses (top),
or the offices of Dr. T. Goldman of Harley Street (bottom)]

125

Just to the north of New Square is a *cul-de-sac* called Stone Buildings constructed to the severely classical designs of Sir Robert Taylor and faced with stone (hence the name). The south wing was added in 1845. William Pitt the Younger had his chambers here, as did Mr. Wharton in Anthony Trollope's *The Prime Minister*. The tradition continues today with most of the occupants belonging to the legal profession. In episode 4.8 it becomes the busy London street – complete with an omnibus (though goodness knows where it was going given that it is a dead end) – where Lady Mary goes to visit the Lotus Club in search of Jack Ross with the intention of asking him not to marry Lady Rose. In the event it is a somewhat wasted trip as Jack has already decided to call off the engagement.

Earlier in episode 4.5 Stone Buildings appears as the location, supposedly in Harley Street, where Lady Edith gets out of the taxi (with the same omnibus in the background) and enters the offices of Dr. T. Goldman having discovered that she is pregnant by Michael Gregson. This seems to be a popular location for doctors for it also where in episode 6.2 Dr. Ryder has his consulting rooms, and to where Anna Bates is brought by Lady Mary in the hope of helping her not have another miscarriage. Stone Buildings (supposedly Eaton Place this time according to the street sign), the taxi and omnibus make yet another appearance in episode 4.7 when Lady Rose, Lady Edith and Lady Rosamund are walking down the street and where after Lady Rose has gone off to do some 'errands' (though she is actually off boating with Jack Ross) Lady Rosamund asks Lady Edith what it is that is worrying her. Stone Buildings (along with the ubiquitous omnibus) also appears in the following series, episode 5.6, as the street in which the hotel to which Lady Edith takes Marigold is situated. Finally it makes a rather out of place appearance in episode 6.8 as the establishing shot for the offices of *The Sketch* which should have been around the corner in New Square. Not surprisingly all the shots of Stone Buildings for the series were done on the same day, and utilised the same vehicles.

Over the last ten years there have been nearly fifty productions shot in the area including *New Tricks*, *Judge John Deed*, *Poirot*, *Whitechapel*, *Miss Marple*, *Foyle's War*, *Garrow's War* and *Parade's End*. On the big screen it can be spotted in *Sherlock Holmes* (2009), *The Wolfman* (2010) and *Sherlock Holmes: A Game of Shadows* (2011). In large part it is the fact that this is a relatively quiet location, which is easily secured and has sufficient parking for an entire film crew right in the centre of London that makes it so popular with production companies.

To the east of Temple Underground station are the Inns of Court, so called since the word Inn has always had a special meaning of mansion or town house, in particular one used for barristers or students. Today there are four

Inns of Court, namely Lincoln's Inn, the Middle Temple, the Inner Temple and Gray's Inn. Each is termed a Honourable Society and not incorporated under any law and are thus self-governing. Each Inn is governed by Benchers (Masters of the Bench) who have the exclusive power to call students to the Bar. Lincoln's Inn is the oldest with records dating from 1422, with the others being established during the 16th century. It was King Edward I who in 1292 gave the monopoly of practice in the courts to persons selected by judges. A legal education at an Inn could take up to seven years to complete during which time the student not only learnt about the law, but was also instructed in music, dancing and history so that they might play their part in high society. After the Civil War the educational aspects of the Inns declined, but a revival took place during the 19th century with the setting up of the Council of Legal Education in 1852, though it was not until 1872 that Bar students first had to sit an exam. Presently there are around 12,000 practicing Bar members.

**[Lincoln's Inn Fields is periodically invaded by large numbers
of white vans as film crews take over the whole area]**

In the second half of the 12th century the Knight's Templar built a residence in the area known as Temple, and began work on the round church. After their suppression in 1312 their property was passed to the Knights Hospitallers who leased part of it to lawyers for use as a hostel. They in

127

turn were suppressed in 1539 with their property passing to the Crown. It was King James I who granted ownership of the Temple to the Benchers in 1609, which in 1732 was split into Middle Temple and Inner Temple.

[Middle Temple Lane looking north towards Fleet Street]

Among the fine buildings at the Inns of Court are the hall, library, gateway, Dr. Johnson's Buildings, King's Bench Walk, Mitre Court Buildings, Temple Gardens Building, Temple Lane and Pump Court. As far as *Downton Abbey* is concerned the Inns of Court keep popping up all the time, although several locations in Middle Temple deserve a special mention. The first is Middle Temple Lane, a cobbled street, which runs down hill from Fleet Street to the Embankment. It is here in episode 4.7 that Lady Edith, accompanied by Lady Rosamund, is seen alighting from a taxi and going into offices in Temple Gardens, which are, in fact, those of Dr. Thompson, an abortionist. While in the waiting room Lady Edith has a change of heart (maybe to secure the plotline in series 5 and 6) and says that it has "… been a mistake" and decides to keep her child. It is also up Middle Temple Lane that the Countess of Grantham and Simon Bricker stroll following their dinner at the Ritz Hotel (page 91) in episode 5.3.

Finally in episode 6.6 this is where Lady Mary and Henry Talbot stroll after their dinner at the Criterion (page 104) – a stroll that ends with them kissing while taking shelter from the rain.

[Thresher and Glenny in Middle Temple Lane]

In episode 4.8 Tom Branson drives Isobel Crawley to Thirsk and parks close to Brick Court in Middle Temple Lane. They agree to meet in ten minutes at the bookshop, so Tom goes off to Bettys tearooms, but on entering he sees Lady Rose and Jack Ross, so thinks better of it and retreats before being spotted. The actual location of Bettys in this instance is the premises of Thresher and Glenny on the corner of Middle Temple Lane and Fleet Street. The company was founded in the 17th century, and specialises in bespoke tailoring, legal wear, gowns and accessories. In fact, they are the oldest Royal Warrant holder, and are currently warranted to Queen Elizabeth II for their renowned shirts.

Bettys has more than one outlet in Middle Temple for it was Essex Court that the security office was transformed into their York tea rooms. It is here in episode 5.5 that Lady Rose meets Atticus Aldridge for the first time as she is struggling in the doorway with her bags of cakes she has bought for the Russian refugees she is helping. Bettys (with no apostrophe) is actually an existing business that was first established in 1919 in Harrogate as a

129

Swiss confectioners. Since then Bettys has expanded and now has six tea rooms, including one in York, but not in Thirsk, where afternoon tea of patisseries, fancies and cakes from the past are served by waitresses dressed in period costumes.

[The security office was the site of Bettys tearoom in York (top), while the cloisters where Atticus and Lady Rose take shelter (bottom)]

[The round church where Russian refugees may be found in the crypt. To the left in the upper picture is the Cloisters Building]

131

Atticus and Lady Rose then walk together to the Cloisters Building where they take shelter from a thunderstorm. There were cloisters here until 1612 when they were built over, but this building was destroyed by fire in 1688 with the resultant new structure, designed by Christopher Wren, being much larger. However, the current structure only dates from just after World War II when it was constructed under the supervision of Sir Edward Maufe, and hence would not have been in existence at the time *Downton Abbey* is set.

From here they cross to Temple Church, which doubles as St. Mary Magdalene in York, where the Russian refugees are staying. The Knights Templar built the first church on this site in 1162, and in 1185 their Great House and round church (based most likely upon the Holy Sepulchre in Jerusalem or the Dome on the Rock) was added. The church is a fine example of the Transitional style with the new pointed arch being cleverly used with the interlacing semicircular of the Romanesque. The inside is quite lavish due to the use of Purbeck marble, and is certainly not the gloomy interior seen in *Downton Abbey*. In 1682 Christopher Wren was called upon to 'beautify' the church with the result that the battlements and buttresses, which serve no structural purpose, were added.

When the Dowager Countess and Isobel Crawley visit the crypt to see Prince Kuragin in episode 5.4 they are first seen walking down Middle Temple Lane before entering the church, with the former vowing to take a taxi back to the station.

Of course the Inns of Court are no stranger to filming and can be seen in various legal dramas from *Rumpole of the Bailey* to *Silk*, *Judge John Deed* and *Crime and Punishment*. In part because of the quiet location they can also be spotted in *Shakespeare in Love* (1998), *Elizabeth* (1998), *The Mummy Returns* (2001), *Bridget Jones: The Edge of Reason* (2004), *The Wolfman* (2010), *Pirates of the Caribbean: On Stranger Tides* (2011), *Great Expectations* (2012), *Closed Circuit* (2013), *Belle* (2013), *Mission Impossible – Rogue Nation* (2015), and, perhaps, most famously in *The Da Vinci Code* (2006) where Temple Church had a central role.

Finally back at Temple Underground Station is Temple Place, which forms a loop around the station joining the Victoria Embankment either side of it. At the eastern end, close to Middle Temple Gardens, is No. 2 Temple Place, which until recently was better known as Astor House. It was built in 1895 by John Loughborough Pearson for William Waldorf Astor, founder of the Waldorf Astoria in New York, but not as a residence for it was always intended to be the Astor Estate Office (though it did have a flat above the office for Lord Astor's private use). The building is in the Early

Elizabethan style and is constructed entirely from Portland stone, with some ornate exterior carvings by Nathaniel Hitch. Looking above the machicolated parapets is a weather vane depicting the *Santa Maria* in which Columbus discovered America. It deliberately symbolised the linking of the United States and Europe, and hence the path of discovery of his ancestor John Jacob Astor who made his fortune from the fur trade and property investments in America.

[**No. 2 Temple Place has been described as one of the loveliest houses in London, and certainly the perfect venue for a Society wedding**]

133

**[The main staircase on which the Marquess of Flintshire gives
Lady Rose some comforting words just prior to her marriage]**

The interior is in the French Renaissance style by John Diblee Crace, who
was also responsible for Astor's main property at Cliveden in
Buckinghamshire. Of particular note are some of the walls, which are
panelled with precious woods and the ceilings which are gilted in gold. The
interior is not to everyone's taste and has been described by Donald
Strachan as having a 'strange Victoriana-meets-Disney vibe' on account of
some of the choices of decoration. For instance on the banisters of the main
staircase characters from *The Three Musketeers* (Astor's favourite book)
can be found, while in the Great Hall there is a gilded frieze with fifty-four
seemingly random characters from history including Pocahontas,
Machiavelli, Bismark, Anne Boleyn and Marie Antoinette. Irrespective of
style No. 2 Temple Place is certainly opulent. It did suffer bomb damage
during World War II, but was fully restored between 1949 and 1951

The Astors sold the property in 1919 after which it was owned in turn by
Sun Life of Canada, the Society of Incorporated Accountants and Auditors
and from 1960 it became the headquarters of Smith and Nephew. Presently
it is owned by the Bulldog Trust, and from 2011 has been open as an art
gallery to the public from January to April each year. Admission is free as
the aim of the trust is to showcase publicly owned art from regional
collections throughout the country. Two Temple Place is also one of
London's hidden gems for corporate and private events, as well as a
stunning setting for central London weddings.

[The Great Room where Lady Rose and Atticus Aldridge marry (top),
and the Clayton and Bell stained-glass window (bottom)]

135

In *Downton Abbey* episode 5.8 No. 2 Temple Place becomes Caxton Hall for the marriage of Lady Rose and Atticus Aldridge, with almost the whole family in attendance. The real Caxton Hall dates from 1878 and is a red brick and pink sandstone affair that became Westminster Town Hall in 1883. It was originally used for concerts and public meetings such as those of the Suffragette movement. During World War II it was used by the Ministry of Information as a venue for press conferences. Today it has been redeveloped as offices and luxury flats. However, it is, perhaps, best known for its Registry Office where Donald Campbell, Billy Butlin, Elizabeth Taylor, Diana Dors, Peter Sellers, Roger Moore, Orsen Wells, Joan Collins, Yehudi Menuhin, Adam Faith, Barry Gibb and Ringo Starr are among the famous that were married here.

It is in the Great Hall that Lady Mary comments to the Dowager Countess that it must be a first for her to be at a wedding in a registry office. Violet will have none of it and recalls that in 1878 she was at a similar ceremony for Lord Roseberry and Hannah Rothschild, though she admits that in "marrying a Rothschild there are certain compensations". Meanwhile Lady Flintshire in a last desperate attempt to stop the wedding announces to all that she and Shrimpie are in the process of getting a divorce. However, her plan fails due to the good sense of Lady Sinderby. Very much in shot while all this high drama is going on is the magnificent Clayton and Bell stained-glass window depicting a Swiss landscape.

Good use is also made of the main stairway as the Marquess of Flintshire escorts his daughter to the Great Hall, giving her some comforting words on the way.

DOWNTON ABBEY IN NORTHUMBERLAND

ALNWICK - ALNWICK CASTLE

[Alnwick Castle is known to millions as the location of Hogwarts in the first two Harry Potter films, but the Crawleys pass over this bridge on their visits to Brancaster Castle in the 2014 and 2015 *Downton Abbey* Christmas specials]

Alnwick is a small town close to the North Sea in Northumberland, dominated by Alnwick Castle, the residence of the Duke of Northumberland. The Castle was built following the Norman conquest, and has been renovated and remodelled a number of times. It is a Grade I listed building.

Yves de Vescy, Baron of Alnwick, erected the first parts of the castle in 1096. It was built to defend England's northern border against the Scottish invasions and border reivers. It was besieged in 1172 and again in 1174 by William the Lion, King of Scotland, with William being captured outside the walls during the Battle of Alnwick. In 1309 the castle was bought from Antony Bek, Bishop of Durham, by Henry de Percy, 1st Baron Percy, and it has been owned by the Percy family, the Earls and later Dukes of Northumberland, ever since. The first Percy, Lord of Alnwick, restored the castle, with the Abbot's Tower, Middle Gateway and Constable's Tower still surviving from this period. Between 1403 and 1408 there were several rebellions in which the 1st Earl of Northumberland, his brother the Earl of Worcester and his son Harry Hotspur were all killed.

During the Wars of the Roses the castle changed hands several times. It was held against King Edward IV until its surrender in mid-September 1461, after the Yorkist victory at the Battle of Towton, near York, at which twenty thousand men died. It was re-captured by Sir William Tailboys during the winter, but he in turn surrendered to Hastings, Sir John Howard and Sir Ralph Grey of Heton in July 1462. Grey was appointed captain, but he surrendered after a sharp siege in the early autumn. King Edward IV responded with vigour, and when the Earl of Warwick arrived in November Queen Margaret and her French advisor, Pierre de Breze, were forced to sail to Scotland for help. They organised a mainly Scots relief force, which under Angus and de Breze, set out on 22nd November. Warwick's army, commanded by the experienced Earl of Kent and the recently pardoned Lord Scales, prevented news getting through to the starving garrisons.

As a result the nearby castles at Bamburgh and Dunstanburgh soon agreed terms and surrendered. But Hungerford and Whittingham held Alnwick Castle until Warwick was forced to withdraw when de Breze and Angus arrived on 5th January 1463.

Hence the Lancastrians missed a great opportunity to bring Warwick to battle instead being content to retire, leaving behind only a token force that surrendered the following day. By May 1463 Alnwick was back in Lancastrian hands for the third time since the Battle of Towton, having been betrayed by Grey who tricked the commander, Sir John Astley, into surrender. However, after Lancastrian defeats at Hedgeley Moor and

Hexham in 1464 Warwick arrived before Alnwick on 23rd June and received the castle's surrender the very next day. Thus ended the War of the Roses for Alnwick Castle.

In the 16th century, and in the second half of the 18th century Robert Adam performed many alterations. The interiors were largely in a Strawberry Hill Gothic style not at all typical of his work, which was usually Neo-Classical. However, in the 19th century Algernon, 4th Duke of Northumberland, replaced much of this with less ostentatious architecture designed by Anthony Salvin. Finally, many of the rooms accessible to the public today are those that have been redecorated in an opulent Italianate style during the Victorian era by Luigi Canina.

During World War II, parts of the castle have been used by various educational establishments: first by the Newcastle Church High School for Girls, then, from 1945 to around 1975, as a teacher training college and, since 1981, by Saint Cloud State University as a branch campus, forming part of their International Study Programme.

The castle consists of two main rings of buildings. The inner ring is set around a small courtyard and contains the principal rooms. As the central block was not large enough to contain all the accommodation required in later centuries, a large range of buildings was constructed along the south wall of the bailey, these two main areas of accommodation being connected by a link building. There are towers at regular intervals along the walls of the outer bailey, with around a sixth of the bailey wall having been reduced almost to ground level on the bailey side to open up views into the adjacent park. In fact Alnwick Castle has two parks. Immediately to the north of the castle is a relatively small area straddling the River Aln, which was landscaped in the 18th century by Lancelot Brown, better known as Capability Brown, and Thomas Call; it is known locally as The Pastures. Nearby is the much larger Hulne Park, which contains the remains of Hulne Priory. The castle is still a home for the present Duke of Northumberland, and next to Windsor Castle this is the largest inhabited castle in England.

It should come as no surprise that the castle has been featured many times on both film and television. It has long been a double for Nottingham Castle, appearing in the television series *The Adventures of Robin Hood* in 1955, and later in *Robin of Sherwood* (four episodes), *Robin Hood and the Sorcerer* and most notably on the big screen as the place Kevin Costner reaches, having only arrived in England that morning near the Beachy Head lighthouse, in *Robin Hood: Prince of Thieves* (1991) – quite a feat considering he only had a horse and that you would be hard pressed to make the four hundred mile journey today by car in the time allowed!

Stock footage of the castle from The Pastures even appears to establish Nottingham Castle in *Star Trek: the Next Generation* (1993).

Readers will probably also recognise the castle from *The Black Adder* and period costume pieces such as *The Virgin Queen* (2005*)*, *Becket* (1964), *Elizabeth* (1998), *Ivanhoe* (1982), *Mary, Queen of Scots* (1971), *The Hollow Crown* (2016) and *The Spaceman and King Arthur* (1979). It has even been home to *Count Dracula* in the 1977 television production of the same name. Maybe its most famous appearance though is as Hogwarts in *Harry Potter and the Philosopher's Stone*, and again in *Harry Potter and the Chamber of Secrets*.

Alnwick in its guise as Brancaster Castle has played host to the *Downton Abbey* production crew on two occasions. The first was during filming of the 2014 Christmas special (episode 5.9) which took place over a two week period in July and August that year, while a return was made in July 2015 for the 2015 Christmas special (episode 6.9) – the very last episode of the series. The state rooms, the grounds and the semi-ruined Hulne Abbey all appear in the 2014 filming, while it is the state rooms, ramparts, and the nearby Bow Alley and St. Michael's Parish Hall in Alnwick itself that feature in the 2015 production. The latter becomes the scene of the village meeting at which the Countess of Grantham tells the locals of the plans for the cottage hospital, watched by her very proud husband and Lady Rose.

[The cars are called up to film the arrival of the Crawleys]

[Courtyard and main entrance to the State Rooms]

The first appearance is set during the autumn of 1924 when Lord Sinderby has rented Brancaster Castle from Lord Hexham for a grouse shooting party. The Crawleys travel by train (using both the Bluebell Railway (page 188), and the North Yorkshire Moors Railway (page 197)) with the Dowager Countess commenting to Isobel Crawley on the platform as the train departs from Downton, that it is, "Not what I call a recipe for a peaceful week's shooting". Next the party are seen in two cars on the bridge crossing the River Aln on The Peth, but are then illogically seen entering via the garden entrance at Lion Arch on the other side of the castle.

They enter the state rooms via the lower guard chamber at which point the Earl of Grantham comments, "What a marvellous place this is". Lord and Lady Sinderby greet the Crawleys on the main staircase.

In between these scenes there are some establishing shots of the castle interiors ending in the drawing room where Lord Sinderby addresses his butler, Stowell stating, "So, everything's under control", which is a sure sign that it will not be for very long.

It is in the library that the group then partake of afternoon tea (although Stowell states that tea is usually served in the ante library), and where Stowell is so obviously rude to Branson, at which point Lady Mary decides that something must be done about the butler's snobbish behaviour.

141

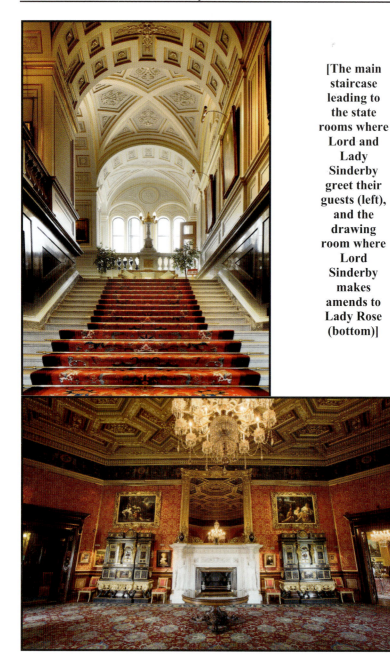

[The main staircase leading to the state rooms where Lord and Lady Sinderby greet their guests (left), and the drawing room where Lord Sinderby makes amends to Lady Rose (bottom)]

[Departure of the shooting party]

The following day the group leave the castle for a shooting party on the moor. Lunch is taken at the semi-ruin of Hulne Abbey in a room with animal skins affixed to the walls. For the evening meal it is back to Alnwick Castle's state dining room.

It is here that Barrow plays a trick on Stowell, having forged a note to the cook saying that Lord Sinderby only requires plain food. This results in Stowell being told by Lord Sinderby to "… conduct yourself more professionally in future", while Barrow is called a "… stupid fool".

The following day there are some beautiful shots of Lady Rose, Atticus, Lady Mary, Branson and Lady Edith walking beside the River Aln with the castle in the background as they discuss the events of the previous night. Prior to dinner that evening the guests are seen gathering for pre-prandial drinks in the saloon.

143

[The state dining room where it is always policy
to serve the master with a full meal]

[After shooting all morning Hulne Abbey provides the location for lunch. On the first occasion it is served in the room with animal skins mounted on the walls to the centre of the picture, while on the second it is served outside with marquees being erected in the picture foreground]

On the third day there is more shooting, and this time lunch is taken in the grounds of Hulne Abbey in the rain. The Abbey was founded in the 13th century by the Carmelites – an order bound by a rule to live in extreme poverty. The priory had a surrounding wall, and from the 15th century a pele tower as well, for it was felt necessary to defend it against any Scots who might come over the border. Today the abbey is part of the several thousand acres comprising Hulne Park, which is part of the Duke of Northumberland's estate and close to the castle. Indeed it was originally a hunting park with woods, moors and stretches of open grassland, and is still used for shooting. Hence all the shooting scenes in the episode are quite authentic. The priory may also be seen in *Robin Hood: Prince of Thieves* (1991) when it doubled as the home of Maid Marian.

Tea that afternoon is in the saloon where Diana Clark, Lord Sinderby's mistress, along with his love-child, appear unannounced, although she has received a telegram in London with an instruction to come. It soon transpires that this is all part of Barrow's revenge on Stowell. In the event

Lady Rose saves the day, and in doing so gains the respect she deserves from Lord Sinderby, who later announces in the drawing room that he now knows that he is lucky to have her as part of the family.

[The saloon – not the place to entertain your mistress (top), while the library (bottom) is not such a quiet place – especially after the installation of a gramophone by Lord Sinderby]

That night Lord Sinderby has had a gramophone installed in the library, much to the appreciation of the younger members of the family who are seen dancing the night away. Most significantly, Lady Mary dances with Henry Talbot, who is seen next day departing early morning in a sports car, which rather impresses her ladyship.

[Setting up for filming in the state rooms]

In the 2015 Christmas special Brancaster Castle is under the ownership of the new Lord Hexham, Bertie Pelham. The Earl and Countess of Grantham arrive by car and this time seem to take a more scenic route to the courtyard, where shortly afterwards they are seen to descend the stairs to the yellow drawing room (which is, in fact, the saloon) where they are greeted by Bertie and his mother. Good use is again made of the drawing room, saloon, library and state dining room, but this time filming also included much more of the exterior with walks being taken along the ramparts.

The Earl of Grantham speaks the truth when talking of the castle he says to Lady Grantham, "You have to admit it's quite something".

147

Brimming with history and magic

From sumptuous State Rooms to Potter-themed tours, a visit to Alnwick Castle fires the imagination.

www.alnwickcastle.com

Alnwick, Northumberland, NE66 1NQ

Alnwick Castle

DOWNTON ABBEY IN OXFORDSHIRE

BAMPTON - ST. MARY THE VIRGIN CHURCH CHURCH VIEW

[Church View, without a war memorial, with the way to the library signposted in the foreground. When filming *Downton Abbey* this is replaced with a prop showing the distances to Ripon and Thirsk. To the left is the house used as Isobel Crawley's home, while to the right is the entrance to the church of St. Mary the Virgin]

The former market town of Bampton, located around 15 miles west of Oxford, on the edge of the Cotswolds near the River Isis, is one of the prettiest and best preserved villages in the country. Many *Downton Abbey* village exterior shots, as well as church interiors, were shot at Bampton.

The name Bampton appears to be part Celtic and part Saxon in origin. The old British suffix 'ton', often spelt 'tune' in old documents, and apparently pronounced 'toon', indicates a high place. It is the original of the modern word 'town'. 'Bam', on the other hand, is from the old English 'beam', meaning a tree, as in 'hornbeam'. The name of the village is variously recorded in ancient documents as 'Beamtunc', 'Beamdune', 'Bemtune' and 'Bentone'.

149

Archaeological evidence indicates that the area was already inhabited during the Iron Age, and subsequently was the site of a large Roman settlement. Although it remained inhabited, Bampton was first mentioned in the Saxon Chronicle, in the record of a battle in A.D. 614. Such occurrences were not rare in that period from the 6th century to the 9th, as what is now Oxfordshire lay between the kingdoms of Mercia and Wessex. The town and its market are listed in the Domesday Book, William the Conqueror's great survey of England in 1086. The origins of the market are not recorded, but the right to hold it would only have been granted if the lord of the town was particularly important to the king.

In 1314-15, the Earl of Pembroke received a licence to 'make a castle of his house at Bampton'. Although the castle was demolished at some period before 1789, parts of the west gatehouse and curtain wall still survive incorporated within a large farmhouse called Ham Court.

Before telephone numbers consisted only of numbers, places were identified by their exchange name – and in Bampton's case, the exchange name was Bampton Castle. A nearby R.A.F. communications station still retains this name.

Bampton was split into different manors over the centuries, and therefore has several manor houses. From the 13th century onwards, the nearby towns of Witney and Burford outgrew Bampton both in population and industry, leaving Bampton as something of a rural backwater.

In 1645, Oliver Cromwell attacked a strong party of Royalists, who had set themselves up in a 'pretty strong house' at Bampton – probably Bampton Castle – but gave in to superior numbers after a siege. Between 1650 and 1750, many substantial houses were built in Bampton, and the market was revived in 1776.

By the early 19th century, the gap between the wealthy landowners and the agricultural workers had widened, and the plight of the poorest became desperate. The building of the town hall in 1838 failed to boost the revival of the weekly market, which after a few years ceased completely. In 1851, there were ten public houses in Bampton.

In 1873, Bampton became connected to the railway network. The station was actually closer to Brize Norton, but it offered travel to London in little more than two hours. This brought more outsiders into town, and old structures slowly changed – Bampton finally got its first street lighting, paid for by voluntary contributions from the newcomers. By the 1950s the number of pubs in the village had risen to thirteen.

[Scene of many a *Downton Abbey* funeral, wedding and christening]

Today, the Bamptonians have five public houses, and a variety of shops offering most requirements. Their pride, however, is the church of St. Mary the Virgin, located at the very heart of the village. The church stands on the site of an Anglo-Saxon Minster, built no later than 950, which was probably destroyed during the siege of Bampton in 1142. All that remains of the old church is the Anglo-Saxon tower with its fine pre-conquest herringbone stonework. The present building was begun in 1153, and remodelled in 1270, when the aisles were added and the spire placed on the tower.

The church was originally dedicated to John the Baptist, and later to St Beornwald, who may have founded the minster. Certainly the building held

151

the shrine of St Beornwald until its destruction during the Reformation. The change of dedication to St. Mary the Virgin is not quite the last, since in *Downton Abbey* it is the church of St. Michael and All Angels.

[Downton church is a place of high drama being witness to weddings, funerals, christenings and even a jilting at the altar in the case of Lady Edith and Sir Anthony Strallen]

The church is built on a cruciform plan with an elegant octagonal central spire crowning the square tower, supported by miniature saint-topped flying buttresses. It is a fine example of the transitional period from Early English to Decorated style.

Visitors like to look for the two Green Man faces on the south doorway, with leaves growing from their mouths. The church was restored in 1870, and today offers 503 seats. The churchyard was closed to new burials in 1898, and is allowed to overgrow during the summer months to encourage wildlife. A new churchyard was consecrated in 1899. The building now enjoys Grade I listed protection.

The church was, of course, the scene for the wedding of Lady Mary and Matthew Crawley in episode 3.1, the Catholic christening of baby Sybil in episode 3.2 (at which Lady Cora, noticing the Earl of Grantham's unease during the photographs, quips, "What's the matter, Robert? Are you afraid you'll be converted when you're not looking?"), the jilting of Lady Edith at the altar in episode 3.3, and the final resting place of Matthew Crawley in episode 4.1 – a memorial to which Lady Mary returns in episode 6.8 to ask for Matthew's approval to marry Henry Talbot. Lady Mary's bridal dress design was kept a secret until filming started properly; Michelle Dockery waited in a carriage, surrounded by crew members holding up umbrellas. Although several walking scenes have been shot near the church, it remains one of the few Bampton locations that have provided interior shots for the series. Most recently it was the scene of a string of marriages in quick succession – Charlie Carson and Elsie Hughes (episode 6.3), Lady Mary and Henry Talbot (episode 6.8) and finally Lady Edith and Bertie Pelham (episode 6.9).

In the church entrance, *Downton Abbey* fans will be pleased to discover the collection of pictures taken backstage during filming, alongside those from *The Suspicions of Mr Whicher*, which was also shot here.

Church View appears in virtually every episode. It is the centre of Downton village, where the Ripon to Pickering bus stops to pick up and set down passengers.

This is also where the eagle-eyed viewer will spot a piece of set dressing in the form of a sign post indicating that Downton is 9 miles from Ripon and 6 miles from Thirsk. From these two pieces of information it is possible to calculate the exact location of the village. The distances alone offer two possible sites, but when the bus service is taken into consideration, assuming that it would travel the most direct route, following the path of the current A61 and A170, the true location of Downton is revealed as the village of Ainderby Quernhow, just off the A61. It is exactly 8.6 miles from Ripon and 6.3 miles from Thirsk. Church View provides the viewer with a cavalcade of vintage cars, charabancs, horses and carts and lorries as people come and go and villagers go about their business.

**[Church View where the Downton fair was held,
and later the war memorial erected]**

It has a more substantial appearance in episode 1.4 as the site of the fairground, which included a fantastic helter-skelter, which the local children were permitted to use for free. This setting was filmed both by day and night. When not required for filming the green makes a convenient assembly point for the crew. However, it is most notably the location of the war memorial (along with the wall plaque to Mrs. Patmore's nephew) unveiled in episode 5.8.

Just a few metres from the church gate is the aptly named Churchgate House – this provided the exterior shots for Matthew's mother, Isobel Crawley's house, although the interior shots were all filmed at West Wycombe House (page 29).

Continuing along Church View, away from the church and Isobel Crawley's house, is the entrance to Bampton Library, formerly the town grammar school. Good use is made of the gate to the right of the library, which serves as the entrance to the cottage hospital, through which many a character can be seen passing in virtually every episode.

[Two views of Churchgate House, the home of Isobel Crawley]

[Entrance to Downton cottage hospital (top), while the lane at the side (bottom) is where Thomas Barrow stores his black-market goods, and where Mrs Patmore's bed and breakfast is located]

The lane at the side of the library was often used as a backdrop, as is the house at the end of it on the left. This is also where, in episode 2.7, Thomas has the lock-up where he stores his black-market goods. Finally close to here may be found the location of Mrs. Patmore's bed and breakfast establishment in episode 6.7.

[The building used as Downton Post Office. Note the dog-waste bin, drain pipes and television aerials to the side of the building, as well as the lack of telegraph wires and shop signage]

The house on the corner of the lane and Church View became Downton Post Office, from which in the very first episode the telegraph boy begins his cycle ride towards the manor house, to deliver the devastating telegram informing the Earl of Grantham that the *RMS Titanic* has sunk, killing the heir to the family estates. However, viewers intending to post a letter will not find any post box at the side of the building – it was only a hollow prop. But it didn't just add to the authentic look of a post office (along with the 'Picture Postcards' sign): it also had a practical use since it covered up a rather too modern item – a red dog-waste bin attached to a footpath signpost. When making a period drama such as Downton Abbey all manner of objects need to be covered, or disguised, such as the black drainpipe to the side of the building, which was clad with wood to make it inconspicuous to the casual observer. The bane of most producers is the television aerial, which must be removed either physically, or digitally in post-production. For the opening shots in that first episode wires, with appropriate insulators, had to be erected across the street, connecting the post office to the telegraph network.

[The Grantham Arms is situated opposite the church of
St. Mary the Virgin in Church View]

158

Church View is well served for public houses since there are two a hundred metres or so from each other. The Grantham Arms, opposite the church, is where Tom Branson lodges for a short time after being dismissed from his post as chauffeur in episode 2.8. It is also where Lord Grantham goes to offer Branson money to leave the estate and Lady Sybil – an offer he refuses. It makes a further appearance in the Christmas 2012 special, set two years later in 1921, as the place where the new maid Edna, who has eyes for the recently widowed Branson, 'accidentally' runs into him, having heard that he would be there at lunchtime. Later in the episode she tells Carson that she cannot work on a particular afternoon as she has made plans to see Branson. This statement seals her fate, as it convinces Carson that she must be dismissed in order to avert another possible scandal. Next door to the Grantham Arms is the home of Sarah Bunting as seen in episode 5.5 when Branson comes to wish her well as she departs Downton.

[The Dog and Duck minus its public house sign]

159

The second public house is the Dog and Duck, where Carson meets with Charles Grigg (episode 1.2). He had worked with Carson as one half of a music hall double act called The Cheerful Charlies. When he unexpectedly arrives in Downton seeking to extort money from Carson, Grigg says that they were rather more than just colleagues: "We're like brothers, him and me" – to which Carson replies, "We are not like brothers!" (with emphasis being placed on the word not).

CHARLBURY - DITCHLEY PARK

![The front entrance to Ditchley which became Mallerton Hall]

[The front entrance to Ditchley which became Mallerton Hall]

Charlbury is a town in the Cotswolds nestling in the Evenlode Valley to the west of the county. Close to here is Ditchley Park. The estate was once the site of a Roman villa and later became a royal hunting ground. The current house dates from the time of George Lee, 2nd Earl of Litchfield who had it built in 1722 to a design by James Gibbs – architect of St. Martin-in-the-Fields in London, and the Radcliffe Camera in Oxford. The interior was richly decorated by William Kent and Henry Flitcroft.

In 1933 Ditchley was purchased by Anglo-American Ronald Tree and his wife, the celebrated interior designer Nancy Lancaster. She was said to have 'the finest taste of almost anyone in the world', and she brought her talents to Ditchley having it restored sympathetically. A frequent visitor to the house was Winston Churchill, particularly during World War II since the house was not easily spotted from the air and had a lack of visible access roads, unlike Chartwell (the Churchill family home) and Chequers (the official country retreat of Prime Ministers). After the war and the subsequent break up of Tree's marriage he sold the property to the tobacco importing family W. D. Wills of Bristol. It was in 1958 that Wills set up a trust called the Ditchley Foundation with the aim of promoting international relations, particularly the understanding of Britons and North Americans. The foundation is still active today via a series of monthly conferences, and welcomes researchers and students who may wish to access the house and its small collection of art.

The house may be seen in *Downton Abbey* episode 6.1 as Mallerton Hall where Sir John Darnley is selling the house and contents by auction, much to the shock of his long time friend the Earl of Grantham. It can also be spotted in *The Young Victoria* (2009) as Buckingham Palace.

KINGSTON BAGPUIZE - KINGSTON BAGPUIZE HOUSE

[The home of Lord Merton]

161

Around 6 miles to the west of Abingdon is the village of Kingston Bagpuize. It was originally just Kingston, but after the Norman Conquest the surname of Ralph de Bachepuise, a French nobleman was added. The village has a fine church dating from 1800 (though it was refurbished in 1882, and extended in 2000), and during World War II there was a satellite airfield for RAF Abingdon just to the east.

The estate dates from 1542 when John Latton purchased the three estates of Kingston Bagpuize. There was already a manor house of sorts on the site. In turn his 9-year-old son inherited the estate in 1622 when the manor house was little more than a moated farm. He set about building Kingston House between 1660 and 1670 at which time it was sold to Edmund Fettiplace. His daughter married John Blandy and the Blandy family owned Kingston House right up until 1917, when Edward Anthony Strauss bought it.

Just like Downton Abbey the village was largely owned by the 'Lord of the Manor'. Strauss was the head of a London firm of grain and seed merchants, and also the Minister of Parliament for North Berkshire. However, in 1935 Strauss & Co. Ltd. went bankrupt with the Kingston House estate, including most of the village, being sold at auction. Lord Ebury bought the house and surrounding parkland, but sold it in 1939 to Miss Marlie Raphael, who was the great aunt of Virginia Grant's late husband, Francis who is the current owner.

What visitors see today is a 1660s manor house that was remodelled in the early 1700s in red brick with stone facings. Inside there is a magnificent cantilevered staircase, and some finely proportioned panelled rooms. The house appears in series 5 and 6 of *Downton Abbey* as the home of Lord Merton.

ROTHERFIELD GREYS - GREYS COURT

Situated on the edge of the Chilterns, just 3 miles from Henley, Greys Court is a picturesque Tudor manor house at the centre of an estate comprising some 280 acres of formal gardens, woodland, parkland and common land. Most of the estate falls into the Chilterns Area of Outstanding Natural Beauty. Despite being a National Trust Property, it is often one of the somewhat forgotten tourist attractions in Oxfordshire.

Greys Court has 14th century fortifications, a beautiful courtyard, ornamental gardens with old-fashioned roses, a wisteria walk and a maze, all set within its medieval walls. There is also a rare Tudor donkey wheel and the remains of a medieval tower dating back to 1347.

The name derives from the Grey family, descended from the Norman knight Anchetil de Greye. The manor of Rotherfield Greys is specifically mentioned in the Domesday Book. The house itself has some fascinating associations with Elizabethan court intrigues. At one time Greys Court was owned by Sir Francis Knollys, treasurer to Queen Elizabeth I, and jailer of Mary, Queen of Scots. Another family member, William Knollys, is said to have been Shakespeare's inspiration for Malvolio in *Twelfth Night*.

[Downton Place, the secondary property to which the Grantham family may have been forced to move, and where the family picnic took place on the lawn in front of the house]

The house was rescued from total neglect by Sir Felix Brunner and his wife Elizabeth Irving, granddaughter of the great actor-manager Sir Henry Irving. They bought the estate and set about rebuilding work in 1937. In 1969 they donated the property to the National Trust, though the family remained in residence until the death of Lady Brunner in 2003.

Greys Court can be seen as Downton Place in episode 3.3, as Lord Grantham prepares to advertise Downton Abbey for sale, following news of his disastrous Canadian investments. The Granthams take a family party to what might become their new down-sized home, Downton Place, and are seen having their picnic on the front lawn with the house in the background. No internal scenes were shot at Greys Court during the three days of filming.

The house will also be familiar to viewers of *Midsomer Murders* in which it has appeared three times (*Dead Man's Eleven*, *Orchis Fatalis*, and *A Sacred Trust*). Most recently it has featured in the *Agatha Christie's Poirot* episode *Elephants Can Remember*, in which it was one of the locations Ariadne Oliver visits while investigating the suspicious deaths of General Ravenscroft and his wife.

For further visitor information see www.nationaltrust.org.uk/greys-court.

SHILTON - THE OLD FORGE

[The picturesque ford and Old Forge at Shilton, which became the Red Lion public house in the Yorkshire village of Kirbymoorside]

The parish of Shilton lies just east of the Roman road known as Akeman Street, but there is little evidence that there was any kind of settlement in the area until a Saxon enclosure, or 'tun', was recorded shortly before the Norman Conquest as belonging to the Godwin family. Along with the other property of Harold Godwinson – the King Harold who was killed at the Battle of Hastings – it was appropriated by William the Conqueror, and as Crown land it was not recorded in the Domesday Book.

In 1203 King John planned to give, amongst others, his manor of Great Faringdon, which included the village of Shilton, to the Cistercian monks. Once the monks eventually established themselves at Beaulieu Abbey in Hampshire the endowment was duly made in around 1205. At this time the only stone buildings in the village would have been the church, barn and grange, all the other houses being constructed of wood or wattle-and-daub. The village remained the property of the Cistercians, although it is unlikely that there were ever any monks in residence, until 1538, when King Henry VIII dissolved the monasteries and seized their assets.

Today Shilton, with its many buildings of local Cotswold stone, remains largely unspoiled, and it has also, most unusually, retained the meadows that sweep down to the heart of the village. Shilton has deservedly been awarded Conservation Area Status. The legacy of the Cistercian monks survives in the tithe barn (now Headford House), the grange (now the Old Manor), the dovecote, the stewpond, and the water meadow.

Another distinctive feature is Shill Brook, which flows through the centre of the village on its way from Burford to Black Bourton (where it becomes Black Bourton Brook) eventually feeding into the River Thames. Next to the Old Forge the brook may be crossed via the picturesque narrow stone bridge or the adjacent ford. Now an attractive cottage, the Old Forge was, as its name suggests, formerly a smithy dating from the 17th century. In *Downton Abbey*, however, it featured as the Red Lion public house in Kirbymoorside, where Bates was found working as a barman in episode 2.4.

SWINBROOK - THE SWAN INN

Swinbrook, about 2 miles to the east of Burford, was at one time on the edge of the Wychwood Forest, where pigs were permitted to graze. The name of the village no doubt reflects the fact that the animals drank at the brook and wallowed themselves in the cool water

The little Swine Brook flows down a narrow valley from the Seven Springs a couple of miles to the north, and is fed by water from a number of other springs on its way down to Swinbrook, where it merges with the River Windrush. In the centre of the village the brook passes through an attractive little wooded area, made enchanting in the spring by wild daffodils and tulips, before moving on to join the Windrush.

[Lady Sybil and Branson stay at the Swan Inn as they endeavour to elope to Gretna Green]

On a vantage point above the village is the parish church of St. Mary the Virgin, which is reached by a set of steps just along the road from the village hall. The church dates from around 1200, and the unusual open-sided bell-tower was added in 1822. Inside, the most notable features are the 17th century wall-tombs of members of the Fettiplace family, landed gentry of Norman descent. Six of them are shown in effigy, rather uncomfortably reclining, in three tiers near the altar. There is also a simpler and more poignant memorial to the crew of the submarine HMS P514, originally the USS R-19, transferred to the Royal Navy in March 1942 under the terms of Lend-Lease. On her maiden voyage as a Royal Navy vessel the submarine was sunk by a Canadian minesweeper after failing to identify herself in thick fog. Her commanding officer was Lieutenant W. A. Phillimore, whose parents lived in the village. David

Freeman-Mitford, 2nd Baron Redesdale, had Swinbrook House built just the north of the village, and four of his six daughters are buried in the cemetery: the novelist Nancy Mitford and her sisters Unity, Diana and Pamela.

To the south of the village, beside the bridge over the River Windrush, is a former flour mill and next to that is the Swan Inn, which is owned by the Dowager Duchess of Devonshire, the last surviving Mitford sister. This is the inn, featured in episode 2.7, where Lady Sybil and Branson stay on their way to Gretna Green. Lady Mary and Lady Edith track them down to a room here, and the former persuades them not to "sneak away like a thief in the night" but instead to return to Downton, at least for a while.

WITNEY - COGGES MANOR FARM

The name of Wyttannige first appears in a Saxon charter of 969, but by the Domesday Book of 1086 it had become Witenie meaning Witta's island. By the Middle Ages a market had been established, and the town had long been an important crossing over the River Windrush. It had become famous for its woollen blankets since this time, and also for beer production after 1841 when J. W. Clinch and Co. founded the Eagle Maltings. In 1861 the town was important enough to have its own railway branch line linking it to Yarnton and Oxford. However, the station was closed in 1970, though there are plans afoot to have the line reopened. The area is known as a safe Conservative seat with former Prime Minister David Cameron being the local Member of Parliament from 2001 to 2016.

The Manor Farm comprises a 13th century manor house along with 17th century farm buildings, both of which are Grade II listed. The first owner, according to the Domesday Book, was named Wadard, a Normal knight who is depicted on the Bayeux tapestry. Later in its history it was Crown property with King Henry VIII giving the land to Thomas Pope, the founder of Trinity College Oxford. But Cogges is much more than a farm museum – it represents the history of a small rural settlement. In the grounds there is evidence of a former moated Norman manor house and earthworks of a shrunken medieval village. There are also the remains of a 12th century priory, and the 13th century manor that was extended to form the present farmhouse. Its traceried lights make very fine kitchen windows.

[Cogges farmyard with stable, along with the wheat and barley barns]

The two large barns pre-date 1725 when cereal production was most profitable. They are well ventilated and constructed of local rubble stone with porches and large rear doorways to allow carts to shelter and unload their wheat and barley. The wheat barn has a stone-flag floor for threshing, while the winnowed grain would have been transferred to a separate granary. Of course, at that time cereal farming was dependent upon horse and oxon-power so there is a small barn for the horses, and a late 18th century byre for the oxon. By the mid-19th century as cereals became less profitable the farm turned over to livestock with the yard being divided up into smaller fold areas along with the weather-boarded cowshed, the open-fronted shelter sheds built against the older stone walls of the yard, the pigsties in the middle of the yard, and finally a small dairy building used to settle the milk and make butter.

As far as *Downton Abbey* is concerned it is the farmhouse kitchen that is of most interest for this was transformed into the set for Yew Tree Farm in series 4, 5 and 6 (though some exterior shots of the farm were also used). In reality the size of the kitchen is far too large for that of a tenant farmer so it had to be shot is such a way so as to make it look smaller. In the production several different farms were used so that when, for instance, Daisy Mason initially visits Mr. Mason at a neighbouring estate this is actually Stockers Farm House in Rickmansworth for the interiors, and Colstrope Farm in Hambleden – also used in the *Midsomer Murders* episode *A Dying Art* – for the rest.

[Entrance (top) and kitchen (bottom) at Yew Tree Farm]

In series 4 (episodes 4.5 and 4.8) Timothy Drewe aspires to take on the tenancy following the death of his father. However, there is a problem in

169

that his father had left behind unpaid debts to the estate, and so Lady Mary and Tom Branson decide to end the lease. Lord Grantham is supportive of the Drewes who have been tenants since the time of King George III, even as far as clearing the debt himself when Timothey Drewe cannot. It is a dilema which is resolved when the Crawleys, just as in real life albeit a half century late, decide that the future is in livestock and give Drewe control of all the estate's pigs.

By series 5 (episodes 5.1 to 5.6) the Drewes are looking after Marigold, Lady Edith's illegitimate daughter and keeping the secret of her parentage. Lady Edith is seen visiting Yew Tree Farm on many occasions to see Marigold much to the irritation of Mrs Drewe. By episode 5.5 the problem has got so bad that Edith is told to stay away from Marigold competely, or that the Drewes will leave the farm. In the following episode this results in Lady Edith deciding to leave and taking Marigold with her, much to the distress of Mrs Drewe. A compromise is reached in episode 5.7 when it is agreed that Marigold can be looked after in the Downton Abbey nursery along with Sybbie and George. That, of course, is not the end of the drama for in episode 6.2 it is Mrs Drewe who takes Marigold back during the Malton Fat Stock Show (page 195), which results in the Drewes having to look for a new tenancy immediately. In episodes 6.5, 6.6 and 6.8 Mr. Mason is now the tenant at Yew Tree Farm as Lady Mary has been persuaded that he will be good with pigs.

Away from *Downton Abbey* Cogges can also be seen in the 2015 series *Arthur & George* about the life of Sir Arthur Conan Doyle.

Cogges hosts filming tours and even has a short film about the making of *Downton Abbey* at the museum for visitors to watch in the main parlour. For visitor information please see www.cogges.org.uk for further information.

DOWNTON ABBEY IN SUFFOLK

AKENHAM - RISE HALL

[View from the British trenches looking across no man's land towards the elevated position of the German lines]

The population of Akenham, 4 miles north-west of Ipswich town centre, numbers only sixty or so, but the site has been inhabited for many centuries. Roman pottery has been found in the fields, as well as a bronze pendant and silver penny from Saxon times. The name Akenham is probably derived from the Old English, indicating that the land belonged to a man called Aca. The village is mentioned in the Domesday Book.

The parish church of St. Mary suffered bomb damage during World War II and was restored in the 1960s. Now disused, it is maintained by the Friends of Friendless Churches. In 1878, however, an incident occurred here that was to occupy the national press for at least a year. Each Sunday the two main landowners, Mr. Gooding of Akenham Hall and Mr. Smith of Rise Hall, would load up their carts and take their employees off to Tacket Street Congregational Church in Ipswich. In fact, nearly all the villagers were non-conformists. Henry Waterman, the sexton, claimed that he was the only Anglican churchman left in the village. The minister in charge of

171

the parish was George Drury, the Rector of Claydon, described today as one of the great high church eccentrics, whose insistence on calling himself Father and celebrating mass scandalised the people of Akenham. Understandably he refused to recognise the election of the Congregationalist Smith as churchwarden, despite the approval of the Bishop of Norwich. Each Sunday he would wait at the church gate, and if anybody turned up he would conduct a service; otherwise, as usually happened, he would return to Claydon. Legally a service required a congregation, not counting the sexton. As Drury held the key, Smith was unable to maintain the fabric of the church, which consequently fell into decay. Another sore point was the fact that, although Drury's stipend for the large parish of Claydon was £240 a year, that for Akenham, whose patron was his own family, was £266.

The ill feeling towards Drury came to a head on the 23rd August 1878 when he went to Akenham in order to bury Joseph Ramsey, the two year old son of a Baptist family, who, since Baptists practise adult baptism, was unbaptised. Consequently the Anglican burial service could not be used. When the coffin arrived it was accompanied by Mr. Smith, Mr, Gooding, with about thirty mourners, and the Reverend Wickham Tozer of the St. Nicholas Street Congregational Chapel in Ipswich. Drury later said that he attempted to take charge of the coffin and accompany it to the grave. The mourners accused him of trying to break up the service. After he stormed off, the coffin was carried through a hedge and buried, which actually broke the Canon Law since it was illegal for a clergyman from another denomination to conduct a service of any kind in an Anglican churchyard. A report in *The East Anglian Daily Times*, which it later emerged had been written by Wickham Tozer himself, claimed that Drury had tried to prevent a Christian burial. It was shortly followed by a spate of letters, including one from Mr. Smith of Rise Hall, who signed it 'A Protestant Churchwarden', accusing Drury of all manner of impropriety. Drury sued for libel but although he won his case he was awarded just forty shillings plus costs. The whole incident sparked intense lobbying of Parliament to change the law, and the Burial Laws Amendment Act was passed in 1880.

The battlefield scenes in series 2 of *Downton Abbey* were filmed on farmland to the rear of Rise Hall, where Kev Smith and Taff Gillingham's company Khaki Devil Ltd. has created a network of authentic replica World War I trenches. This remarkable site has been used in many television productions besides *Downton Abbey*, including *The Last Tommy*, the episode of Channel 4's *Secret History* dealing with *Britain's Boy Soldiers*, *Days That Shook the World*, *Wilfred Owen – A Remembrance Tale*, *Victoria Cross Heroes* and, perhaps most notable of all, *The Somme: From Defeat to Victory*.

[These two pictures illustrate the difference in building methods between the German (top) and British (bottom) trenches]

173

The realism of the site is reflected in the fact that the British trenches are shallower and narrower than the German trenches, which, as they always were, are located on higher ground. The area between is landscaped with shell-shattered trees, barbed wire, scrap metal and the like to represent No Man's Land, complete with shell holes. The trench system was built specifically for film and television, with many of the firebays opened up to allow an unobstructed view. In addition the British line has a listening post, which can also double as a machine gun post, a regimental aid post for stretcher cases, a length of un-revetted communication trench and some basic assembly trenches. The German lines are constructed differently, using mainly split logs, but there is also a damaged section featuring wooden hurdles, and in among the ruins and rubble behind the main trench is a machine gun post. The farmhouse and outbuildings are available for filming, and every June the site becomes even more authentic, when poppies, that enduring symbol of the World War I, burst out in a riot of colour over the whole area.

Rise Hall is private and not open to the public, but should you be interested in further information about this magnificent location please refer to the Khaki Devil web site (www.khakidevil.co.uk). The company also provides a service specifically aimed at schools, amateur dramatic societies and community theatre.

DOWNTON ABBEY IN SURREY

BYFLEET - BYFLEET MANOR

**[Home of the Dowager Countess of Grantham, supposedly in
Yorkshire, but actually located in leafy Surrey]**

Byfleet lies just within the M25, next door to Brooklands, the world's first
purpose-built motor racing circuit, which today houses a motor and
aviation museum. The village may look like a modern commuter suburb,
but the area has been inhabited at least since the Bronze Age. Of the
regrettably few ancient buildings remaining, St. Mary's Church dates from
the 13th century. Among its more unusual features are 14th century wall
paintings and a war memorial constructed from the original wooden grave
markers of Byfleet men who fell in World War I. Notable persons buried
here include motor racing legend J. G. Parry-Thomas, Harold Barnwell, the
first test pilot for Vickers, and Honor Wellby, one of the first British
women pilots to die in an aeroplane crash. Byfleet also has a literary claim
to fame as it features in H. G. Wells's 1898 novel *The War of the Worlds*.

The first written reference to Byfleet was long before this, however, in 727,
when the lands belonged to Chertsey Abbey. In 1086 the Domesday Book
recorded a manor house, mill and church, along with enough forest to graze
for ten hogs. At this time, Byfleet was part of the Forest of Windsor, where

King William I liked to hunt. Thereby, the village became a royal manor, and retained that status until 1826.

The Manor House became a favourite royal country retreat. frequented by King Edward II, who granted it to his notorious favourite, Piers Gaveston, and by Edward the Black Prince, the eldest son of King Edward III. Queen Elizabeth I stayed here in 1576, and in 1617 Queen Anne of Denmark, wife of King James I, had the house rebuilt in grand style. Sadly most of that work has since been demolished, with only two chimney stacks and the gateway to the courtyard surviving. On a literary note, the poet Geoffrey Chaucer often came here in his capacity as Clerk of the Works.

Today Byfleet Manor is a Grade II* listed private residence which can be hired out for various functions as well as filming, and will probably be recognised for its appearances in such productions as *Poirot* and *Cranford*. In *Downton Abbey*, Byfleet Manor features as the Dower House, home of Violet Crawley, the Dowager Countess of Grantham, played so perfectly by Dame Maggie Smith. The main interior location used is the drawing room, and the gardens appear in many exterior scenes, with the celestial sphere sundial on the front lawn invariably featuring in the establishing shots. The location scouts had been instructed to find a Georgian style house, as the producers wanted to place Violet back in the Georgian era, so as to root her in history and tradition. When she speaks with the Duke of Crowborough over dinner, the Dowager Countess refers to her house as a 'little cottage', designed by Wren for the first Earl's sister.

Egham Hill - Royal Holloway

The area predates 666 when Chertsey Abbey was founded with many miles of land, which included that of Ecga's Ham, one of the oldest surviving charters in the country. Today Egham is a town in the Runnymede borough of Surrey around 20 miles from central London. It can be considered a university town as on its higher part, Egham Hill, is the campus of Royal Holloway, University of London. The site was formed by the merger of Royal Holloway College and Bedford College in 1985, the former having been founded by the philanthropist Thomas Holloway for the higher education of women. Its magnificent buildings were designed in the French Renaissance style and set in large grounds, and opened by Queen Victoria in 1886. Bedford College was founded in 1849 to give women a liberal education and took its name from its original location in Bedford Square. In 1880 it became a school within the University of London.

[Founder's Court at Royal Holloway, University of London]

When Royal Holloway College was incorporated into the University of London in 1900, the original bequest of Thomas Holloway included a collection of Victorian paintings, among which are works by Frith, Millais, Fildes, Constable, Turner and Gainsborough. When he first planned his women's college Holloway did not envisage including an art gallery. However, when his brother-in-law visited Vassar College, in New York State, then the world's leading college for women, he reported back that they had a superb collection of art. This inspired Holloway to start buying paintings to form a collection for his students in 1881. It is thought that this was the first collection created in Britain specifically for female viewers.

Holloway's creation of the collection was extraordinary in many ways. For a start he was an octogenarian when he began making his purchases, and all his buying was done within just two years. Most of the collection was bought from Christie's auction house, and in two cases he broke auction house records in order to secure the paintings he had selected for the collection. In total Holloway bought 77 paintings at a cost of almost £84,000. In order to exhibit such a collection a purpose built gallery was constructed to the design of Henry Crossland in the women's recreation room – it remains there to this day. In addition there are other gifts, acquisitions and commissions, as well as the Herringham Collection – after Christiana Herringham who was a mover and shaker in the Edwardian art world.

[The picture gallery housed in women's recreation room]

The college is no stranger to film units and can be seen in such productions as *Howards End* (1992), *Basic Instinct 2: Risk Addiction* (2006) and *Avengers: Age of Ultron* (2015), while on the small screen it pops up in such series as *Midsomer Murders* and *Great British Railway Journeys*. In the last episode of series 4 of *Downton Abbey* (*The London Season*) it is in the picture gallery that Lady Mary and Charles come across Lord Gillingham, Lady Rose and Freda Dudley Ward. This provides an opportunity for the two suitors of Lady Mary to spar verbally with each other, at which point Freda instructs them to "Play nicely children".

For visitor information on the gallery, which is normally open on Wednesdays in the Spring and Autumn terms see the college website (www.royalholloway.ac.uk).

KINGSTON UPON THAMES - COUNTY HALL

The King's Estate, or Kingston, has always been of strategic importance due to the fact that at one time the River Thames was fordable here. Until 1750 a wooden bridge, dating back to pre-Conquest times, was the only structure to cross the river above London Bridge. The current stone bridge dates from 1828. Fishing was also important to the area and explains why

178

there are three salmon embodied in the Kingston coat of arms. Other industries past and present have included brewing, malting, tanning, milling, boat building, aviation, chemicals, engineering, plastics, printing and refrigeration. The royal connection with the borough dates back to a charter granted in 1200 during the reign of King John. In 1628 King Charles I gave the town a charter for a market, forbidding any other market within a seven-mile radius.

[The original clock tower at County Hall]

Buildings of note include Kingston Grammar School (founded by Queen Elizabeth I in 1561), and the Market Hall built in 1838 to the design of Charles Henman. The latter was also the town hall until 1935 when it was replaced by the Guildhall designed by Maurice Webb. Close by is another civic building, the County Hall, opened in 1893. It serves as the administrative centre for Surrey County Council, and befitting its status is adorned by a clock tower and various sculptures. The original building has been extended several times (1930, 1938, 1963 and 1982) and today forms

179

two quadrangles. In July 1944 it was unlucky in being hit by a V1 flying bomb, which destroyed the Ashcombe block (subsequently rebuilt in 1953).

A major function of the original County Hall was as a court and jail. However, since the opening of a new court next door several decades ago the existing rooms have remained empty, or converted to offices. Today the 'Old Court House' may be hired out for weddings and other events, and is often to be seen in television productions where a court or prison cells are required. Among those that have visited are *Endeavour*, *Midsomer Murders*, *Silk*, *Poirot*, *Call the Midwife*, *The Bill*, *Ashes to Ashes*, *Jonathan Creek* and *Silent Witness*. It was for series 3 of *Downton Abbey* that the Old Crown Court was used for the trial scenes of Mr. Bates, though Lincoln Castle (page 53) and Chalfont Campus were used for the prison itself. This was a lonely time for Brendan Coyle, who plays Mr. Bates since virtually all his scenes for the entire series 3 were solo ones away from the main cast. There is also a brief scene here in episode 6.5 when Phyllis Baxter, accompanied by Mr. Molesley, goes to court to be a character witness at the trial of Mr. Coyle.

RICHMOND UPON THAMES - HAM HOUSE

[Ham House – the sleeping beauty among country houses]

Originally just a few cottages and a simple manor house beside the River Thames, Shene did not become important until King Henry VII rebuilt the manor house after a fire in 1497. The new structure, now a palace, he called Rychemonde after his earldom in Yorkshire. Queen Elizabeth I spent her last days here. The 18th century saw the construction of Richmond Bridge and many fine terraces around Richmond Green and Richmond Hill. The latter is adjacent to Richmond Park, the largest of London's Royal Parks and a site of Special Scientific Interest, as well as a Special Area of Conservation. The park, which may be driven through between the hours of dawn and dusk, supports over 600 red and fallow deer.

Ham House, by the River Thames and surrounded by parkland, has survived relatively unaltered since the 17th century. It is best described by John Evelyn who in 1678 wrote in his diary, 'After dinner I walked to Ham to see the House and Garden of the Duke of Lauderdale, which is indeed inferior to few of the best Villas in Italy itself; the House furnished like a great Prince's; the Parterres, Flower Gardens, Orangeries, Groves, Avenues, Courts, Statues, Perspectives, Fountains, Aviaries, and all this at the banks of the Sweetest River in the World, must needs be surprising'.

The house was built in 1610 by Sir Thomas Vavasour and from 1637 was the residence of the Earls of Dysart for nearly 300 years. The 1st Earl, William Murray as a youth was the whipping boy to the future King Charles I. However, the house was considered too small, so in 1672 building work started to double its size. No expense was spared on the interiors with the walls being hung with tapestries, or other rich fabrics such as damask and velvet, and exotic furniture was imported from all over the world. During the time of the 3rd Earl the fortunes of Ham changed to the extent that the house was stripped of its splendour with its treasures being put into storage. In 1935 the property was passed to Sir Lyonel Tollemache, second cousin to the 9th Earl, and in 1948 his son gave it to the National Trust. It is open to the public and boasts a 17th century formal garden, a great rarity since most of the gardens from that time were swept away in the 18th and 19th centuries in favour of more natural landscaping.

It should be no surprise that Ham House has featured in many feature films including *Spice World* (2007), *To Kill a King* (2003), *Cambridge Spies* (2003), *Ballet Shoes* (2007), *The Young Victoria* (2009), *Never Let Me Go* (2010), *John Carter* (2012), *Anna Karenina* (2012), *A Little Chaos* (2014) and *Victoria and Abdul* (2017). Its appearance in *Downton Abbey* is restricted to being used as the kitchen at Crawley House, with the exterior being filmed in Bampton (page 154) and other interiors in Beaconsfield (page 17).

RUNNYMEDE - PRESIDENT HALL

[President Hall became Ripon Register Office in *Downton Abbey*]

The water-meadow of Runnymede, between Old Windsor and Egham, is most famous as the place where King John set his seal to the Magna Carta in 1215, though the exact location is still uncertain. The name is probably derived from the Old English 'runieg mede' meaning a meadow where regular meetings were held. The Witan, or council of the Anglo-Saxon rulers, did indeed convene here from time to time during the reign of Alfred the Great.

Today much of the land is managed by the National Trust, and there are several important memorials to visit. In 1929 Sir Edwin Lutyens was commissioned to design twin lodges and stone piers at the northern end of the meadow, and twin octagonal kiosks with stone piers at the southern end. They celebrate both the sealing of the Magna Carta, and the memory of Urban Hanlon Broughton, whose American-born widow donated this historic site to the nation.

182

Then there is the Air Forces Memorial, which commemorates all the men and women of the Allied Air Forces who died during World War II. It records the names of the 20,456 airmen who have no known grave. The memorial is on high ground at the top of Priest Hill (where, incidentally, the last fatal duel in England took place in 1852) along Cooper's Hill Lane, and from it there are commanding views over Windsor and the surrounding counties, including, most appropriately, Heathrow airport.

Here too we find the British memorial to the assassinated American President John F. Kennedy. Dedicated in May 1965 by Queen Elizabeth II and Kennedy's widow Jacqueline, it consists of a garden in which is a Portland stone tablet inscribed with words taken from the President's Inaugural Address.

Finally there is the Magna Carta memorial itself, situated in a grassed enclosure at the bottom of Cooper's Hill. It is a simple and rather bland domed classical temple enclosing a pillar of English granite, inscribed with the words: 'To commemorate Magna Carta, symbol of Freedom Under Law'. The memorial was created by the American Bar Association and unveiled on the 18th July 1957 at a ceremony attended by American and English lawyers. Over the years other inscriptions have been added to the stone pavement to mark important anniversaries.

Along Cooper's Hill Lane is Cooper's Hill House, which is presently waiting redevelopment. The first known records date from 1160, when Abbot Hugh of Chertsey gave the site to the Priory of Ankerwyke, a house of Benedictine Nuns. Upon the dissolution of the Monasteries King Henry VIII gave the priory to Andrew, Lord Windsor in 1539. It changed hands several times before passing to the Harcourt family in the 18th century, remaining with them until the rogue financier Baron Albert Grant purchased it in 1865.

The lavish parties that Grant held at the house he built there attracted the most illustrious guests, including the Prince of Wales. In 1870, however, following a financial collapse, Cooper's Hill House was sold to the Royal Indian Engineering College, whose President, Sir George Chesney, had happened to see the empty building on the hill while he was boating on the river below. The College occupied the site until 1906, when it moved to India.

Under the direction of Sir Matthew Digby Wyatt, who had worked with Sir Gilbert Scott on the India Office in Whitehall, an entirely new block was constructed, containing classrooms, library, lecture theatre, model room, dining hall, laboratory and sleeping rooms for each of the hundred students (the number was later increased to 150). The President lived in the original house, which was later renamed President Hall. The college was opened in August 1873 by the Duke of Argyll, who has his own *Downton Abbey* connection (page 201).

The grounds are noteworthy for the sheer variety of trees, which were developed from botanical specimens bought back from all parts of the British Empire by engineers taking the forestry courses. Unfortunately many of the larger specimens, including two exception Monkey Puzzle trees, did not survive the storms of 1986 and 1989.

After the college vacated the site, the buildings remained empty until 1911, when the estate was sold to the first Baron Cheylesmore, whose family lived there until 1925, when the third Lord Cheylesmore was killed in a car accident (much the same fate as befell Matthew Crawley). The family retained the estate until 1938, when the London County Council, with some foresight, bought it as an emergency headquarters in preparation for the impending war. The following year various administrative departments moved from County Hall to Cooper's Hill, including motor licensing and some sections of the Education Department. Even the statue of Eros was removed from Piccadilly Circus and stored here in what became known as the Eros Room. After the war the site became an Emergency Training College for teachers, until in 1951 the Shoreditch College of Education was relocated from its campus in Hoxton to Cooper's Hill, where there was room for expansion. It remained there until 1980, when the government decreed a general reduction in teacher training. Only the design and technology courses were retained, and that was achieved by merging the college with Brunel University. The design courses in particular were popular, but rising maintenance costs forced the university to transfer the courses to its main campus in Uxbridge and run down the Cooper's Hill site. In 2007 it was sold to the Oracle Group for £46.6 million. Unfortunately they went into liquidation in 2010, and despite new ownership the site still waits its promised redevelopment.

Its one starring role in *Downton Abbey* is as Ripon Register Office, where Bates and Anna marry in episode 2.8. All that was needed to make the scene look authentic were a couple of signs added to the outside of President Hall next to the main doors.

DOWNTON ABBEY IN WEST SUSSEX

CHICHESTER - GOODWOOD CIRCUIT
WEST WITTERING BEACH

Chichester is a Roman, medieval and Georgian city that is currently the administrative centre for West Sussex. It is known for its 11th century cathedral, the Chichester Festival Theatre, Buttermarket designed by John Nash, the Chichester Cross and for boating activities centred around the marina. Just over a mile north-east of the city is the village of Westhampnett, and to the north of this parish is Goodwood racecourse set high on the South Downs, Goodwood House and most of Goodwood Airfield and motor racing circuit.

Goodwood House is one of the finest in England and home to the Dukes of Richmond and Gordon. The current house was built between 1780 and 1800 in Sussex flint by James Wyatt for the 3rd Duke of Richmond. It contains pictures by Canaletto, Van Dyck, Romney and Lely, sporting pictures by Stubbs and Wootton, furniture of the King Louis XV period and a fine collection of porcelain. He also commissioned Goodwood racecourse which was established in 1802.

[The Goodwood Revival]

The racing circuit, which is also on the estate, began life much later as the perimeter track of RAF Westhampnett, constructed during World War II as

185

a relief airfield for RAF Tangmere. At the first meeting in 1948 Stirling Moss won the 500cc (Formula 3) race. Goodwood became the home of the Glover Trophy non-championship Formula One race, the Goodwood Nine Hours sports car endurance race run in the 1950s (dominated by Aston Martin) and the Tourist Trophy sports car race. Today Goodwood is known for two events – the Goodwood Festival of Speed and the Goodwood Revival. The former is an annual hill climb in the grounds, usually held in late June over a 4-day period and features historic and modern motor-racing vehicles. The Goodwood Revival is a 3-day festival held each September for the types of cars and motorcycles that would have completed on the circuit in the early years up to 1966. Historic aircraft help to complete the vintage feel, with nearly all the visitors dressing up in period clothes. Among the famous who have taken part in the Goodwood Revival are professional drivers such as Stirling Moss, Jack Brabham, David Coulthard, Damon Hill and Barry Sheene, and celebrities including Chris Rea and Rowan Atkinson. There is even a pedal car race for children held for the Settrington Cup.

In *Downton Abbey* episode 6.7 the Crawleys are invited to watch the motor car racing at Brooklands by Bertie Pelham. Unfortunately although Brooklands would have been the correct choice at that time, today it does not have the extent of track required for such filming. Hence it was the Goodwood circuit that was used for all the scenes in the episode, including the crash in which Charlie Rogers and Henry Talbot were involved. It is only now that Lady Mary realises that she has deep feelings for Henry, and as a consequence gives him up (at least for the rest of the episode). In real life it was at Goodwood in 1962 that saw the end of the racing career of Stirling Moss who was badly hurt in his Lotus on the Ford water bend.

Also within the Chichester district is the village of West Wittering on the Manhood Peninsula around 6-miles south-west of the city and close to the mouth of Chichester harbour. Smart estates of substantial houses, many of them on private roads, have grown up behind the old village, centred on the village church. The beach is more than a mile long and is reached down a narrow road from the village ending at a large car park below the dunes.

At its western end, opposite Hayling Island, the beach curves round to form a sickle-shaped area of dunes, sheltering a tidal lagoon on its inner side, and with a shingle bank to the seaward side. This is the 76-acre East Head, a fragile natural environment, under constant attack from both the sea and the pressure of visitors walking round from West Wittering. It is owned by the National Trust with the dunes having been fenced off to allow the marram grass to establish itself. The high water quality makes West Wittering beach one of the premier Blue Flag beaches in the country.

[West Wittering beach where Carson and Mrs Hughes go paddling]

It could have been a very different landscape for in the 1950s the area was owned by the Church Commissioners who were in discussion with the likes of Billy Butlin with plans afoot to build a holiday complex here. The local council would do nothing to intercede so it was left to 126 residents to form the West Wittering Estate Limited. They made subscriptions to the new company and by July 1952 had raised just over £20,000 in order to purchase the land from the Church Commissioners. The aims of the company were simple – 'the preservation of the beach and waters adjoining the company's land for the safe and peaceful enjoyment of the public and the preservation of the rural and undeveloped nature of the company's property and its surroundings'. In 1964 East Head was gifted to the National Trust, and in 1984 an agreement was reached with English Nature to ensure that the land is protected from any form of development. On a summer Sunday there can be as many as 15,000 visitors.

In *Downton Abbey* the beach made the perfect location for the staff outing at the end of episode 4.9 when Carson is seen holding hands with Mrs Hughes as they paddle in the sea together. It was certainly a more popular choice than the suggested visits to the Science Museum, Westminster Abbey or the Royal Institution that Mr. Carson put forward to an unenthusiastic staff while at Grantham House for the 'London Season'. It is

187

implied that the beach in question is that at Brighton. The first clue is when Carson says that they will take the Pullman train from Victoria at a cost of 12 shillings (which the family are happy to pay). This was indeed an expensive trip for the average weekly wage for the staff would have been around 20 shillings. The train they took was probably not the famous Brighton Belle, but the Southern Belle, another all-Pullman train run by the London, Brighton & South Coast Railway and introduced in 1908 with a special day return fare of 12 shillings. At the time it claimed to be 'the most luxurious train in the world'. The second clue is when Carson looks at a postcard of Brighton Beach pinned to the notice board. However, there is are problems with the location as it is clearly not Brighton beach which has no sand, only pebbles, has many buildings along the sea front which would have been in shot, and a distinct lack of sand dunes.

HORSTED KEYNES - BLUEBELL RAILWAY

The Bluebell Railway, the world's first preserved standard-gauge steam-operated passenger railway, actually dates back to 1877, when an Act of Parliament authorised the construction of a line from Lewes to East Grinstead, sponsored by local landowners. The following year another Act allowed the London, Brighton and South Coast Railway to buy and run the line. The Lewes and East Grinstead Railway had six stations, but except for Barcombe they were situated close to the residences of the sponsors. Sheffield Park station, for example, was built for the use of the Earl of Sheffield. Only Barcombe station was within easy reach of a village. The line was intended to be double track throughout, but from Horsted Keynes to Lewes only a single track was laid, with passing loops at the stations. From 1882, when it was opened, the line was rarely profitable, and in 1955 it was closed by British Railways.

Local users challenged the decision, pointing out that the 1877 and 1878 Acts imposed a duty on the line to provide four passenger trains each way every day, stopping at Sheffield Bridges, Newick, and West Hoathly, with through connections at East Grinstead to London. British Railways reopened the line in 1956, with trains stopping at the stations specified, but following a public enquiry the relevant section of the Acts was repealed, and in 1958 the line was finally closed. In 1959 the Bluebell Railway Preservation Society was set up, with the aim of operating a commercial service over the whole line, using an ex-Great Western diesel railcar, but the plan was unsuccessful, as the society was unable to buy the whole line.

**[Platform 2 at Horsted Keynes station was transformed into
Downton station for the television series]**

A more modest proposal was adopted: that the section between Sheffield
Park and Horsted Keynes should be preserved as a tourist attraction, using
vintage stock operated by volunteers. In 1960 the line was opened from
Sheffield Park to Bluebell Halt, just short of Horsted Keynes, where the
station still served the electrified line to Ardingly. Three years later British
Railways closed that line, allowing the Society to take over Horsted
Keynes station. Little by little, sections of the original line were purchased
and re-opened. The extension from Horsted Keynes to Kingscote was
completed in 1994, and the line from Kingscote to East Grinstead opened
in 2013. There are plans to extend southward, eventually connecting with
the main line at Lewes.

For film and television producers, one of the most appealing aspects of the
Bluebell Railway is that the various stations have been restored to represent
different historical periods. Sheffield Park is quintessentially Victorian,
Horsted Keynes embodies the era of the Southern Railway between 1922
and 1948, and at Kingscote we find a British Railways station of the 1950s.

For *Downton Abbey*, Horsted Keynes is the obvious location, although the
props department, despite all their efforts, cannot hide the fact that the
station is painted in Southern Railways green and cream – clear evidence
that this is not part of the network serving Yorkshire. Various arrivals and

189

departures for the entire six series have been shot here, usually on the same day for each series. Most memorable, perhaps, is episode 4.2 when Mr. Carson appears out of the steam to make his peace with Charlie Grigg, his old music hall partner, whom he suspects was responsible for stealing his sweetheart away from him. Honour is satisfied when Carson learns that Anne considered him the better man and always regretted her choice of Charlie. For an account of how such filming takes place see page 5.

[Actors pose for photographs next to props put there the night before by the *Downton Abbey* production crew]

The many films in which the Bluebell Railway has featured include *The Innocents* (1961), John Betjeman's *Metro-land* (1971), Ken Russell's *Savage Messiah* (1972) and *Lisztomania* (1975), *A Room with a View* (1985), *The Wind in the Willows* (1996), *102 Dalmatians* (2000), *Miss Potter* (2006) and *The Woman in Black* (2012). It is also a favourite location for television dramas, such as *The Adventures of Sherlock Holmes*, *Miss Marple*, the 1999 version of *The Railway Children, Foyle's War, Tess of the D'Urbervilles* (2008), and most recently *Endeavour* and *Dancing on the Edge* (2013).

The Bluebell Railway is still run largely by volunteers. Its collection of more than thirty steam locomotives – the largest on any preserved line in the country, and second only to the National Railway Museum – is complemented by almost one hundred and fifty carriages and wagons, most of them dating from before 1939. The Golden Arrow Pullman dining train, comprising the Pullman Cars 'Christine' and 'Lilian', and the British Railways 1674 Restaurant Car, recreates the luxurious service that once linked London and Paris. Prospective visitors should check the railway web site (www.bluebell-railway.com) for details of special events.

[The only way to travel – a Pullman train on the Bluebell Railway]

Finally in episode 5.9, the 2014 Christmas special, the family travel to Brancaster Castle in the autumn of 1924. They set off from Horsted Keynes (Downton) with Mr. Carson reminding Mr. Barrow to make sure that the luggage is transferred correctly in York. In the next shot they are on the North Yorkshire Moors Railway (page 197) travelling across the moors in LNER teak carriages of the 1930s, and being pulled by a locomotive built in 1954. Worse still the interior is not that of a LNER carriage, but quite definitely a Pullman car belonging to the Bluebell Railway – in fact a Pullman kitchen 1st class named *Fingall* built in 1924.

DOWNTON ABBEY IN WILTSHIRE

LACOCK - CHURCH STREET

[Lacock Abbey founded in 1232]

Lacock, close to the town of Chippenham and almost entirely owned by the National Trust, is mentioned in the Domesday Book as having a population of under two hundred persons. It was also said to have two mills and a vineyard. Most important to the village, though, is Lacock Abbey, which was founded on the manorial lands by Ela, Countess of Salisbury in 1232. The village and the manor formed its endowment to 'God and Saint Mary'. Lacock was granted a market and developed a thriving wool industry during the Middle Ages. It was ideally placed for this activity, being situated on a main road to London, and on the River Avon, so that boats could transport its goods to Avonmouth, near Bristol, from where they could continue their journey via ship to all parts of the globe.

During the Dissolution of the Monasteries in 1540 the abbey and estate, which included the village, were sold to William Sharington for the sum of £783. They later passed into the Talbot family by marriage, but not before he had turned the abbey into a private residence, retaining much of the

193

medieval fabric of the house and adding a three-storey octagonal tower, tall Renaissance chimneys, and a stable courtyard.

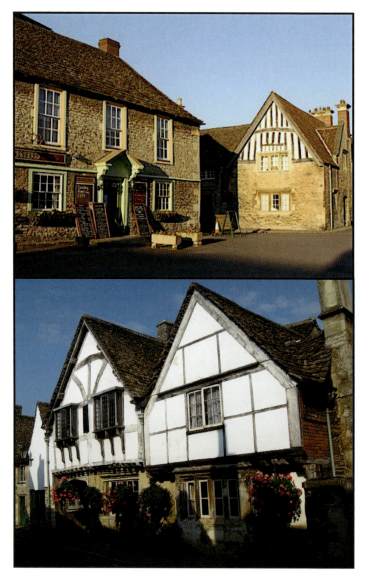

[Buildings in the Church Street – The Carpenters Arms outside of which the Malton Fat Stock Show was filmed (top) and At the Sign of the Angel which has parts dating from the 15th century (bottom)]

In 1916 Charles Henry Fox Talbot bequeathed the Lacock estate to his niece, Matilda Gilchrist-Clark, who took the name of Talbot. The estate, comprising nearly three hundred acres, the abbey, and the village, was given to the National Trust in 1944 by Matilda Talbot. The Talbot family are of course most famous for William Henry Fox Talbot, who made many pioneering contributions to the science of photography, none more so than the invention of the negative/positive photographic process. There is a museum to his work in the abbey.

Today most of the surviving houses in the village are 18th century or earlier in construction. There are a 14th century tithe barn, a medieval church, and an inn dating from the 15th century, as well as an 18th century lock-up. The abbey itself has fine medieval cloisters, sacristy, chapter house, a clock house, brewery and bake house to attract the visitor. Indeed, the whole area remains virtually unspoilt, and this is the prime reason why Lacock can be considered a living film set. Furthermore, because Lacock is under the strict management of the National Trust the buildings do not have television aerials, overhead cables, telephone lines, satellite dishes, or even yellow road lines, which all helps when making period dramas. A director just has to add a little sand over the tarmac roads and a few roaming sheep in order to travel back in time over hundreds of years.

The abbey itself is recognisable on television for appearances in productions such as the 1995 adaptation of *Pride and Prejudice*, *Robin of Sherwood* (four episodes) and *The Mayor of Casterbridge*, while on the larger screen it can be seen in *The Moonraker* (1958), *The Secret of My Success* (1965). *The Other Boleyn Girl* (2008) and in *Harry Potter and the Philosopher's Stone* (2001), *Harry Potter and the Chamber of Secrets* (2002) and *Harry Potter and the Half-Blood Prince* (2009). The latest film to be made in the village is *The Wolfman* (2010).

Most appearances, though, are of the village as a whole, which features prominently in television costume drama productions such as the 2007 series of *Cranford*, *Henry VIII*, *Pride and Prejudice* (both the 1967 and 1995 series), *Robin of Sherwood*, *Tess of the D'Urbervilles* and *Emma*. Indeed, it was Church Street, with St. Cyriac's Church in plain view, that became the scene of the Malton Fat Stock Show – an event which still takes place in some old market towns where livestock is for show and sale with the emphasis being on fattened animals. It features in episode 6.2 of *Downton Abbey* when Marigold goes missing during the show, and is later found with Mrs Drewe leading to her husband agreeing to look for a new tenancy immediately.

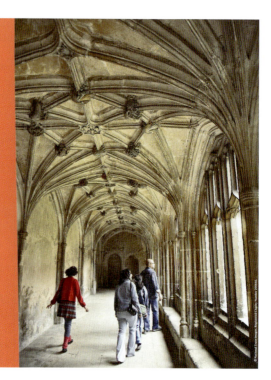

Downton Abbey in Yorkshire

Goathland - North Yorkshire Moors Railway

[Goathland station with a static camping coach behind the shelter]

Goathland is a village with a population of around four hundred people in the North York Moors National Park, situated due north of Pickering, and as such is surrounded by beautiful scenery. The village can trace its roots back to Viking times, and in the 19th century was considered a spa town – which partly accounts for the large number of hotels and guest houses in the area, the largest being the Mallyan Spout Hotel, named after the nearby waterfall. Much of the surrounding land is owned by the Duchy of Lancaster, and the Duchy's black faced sheep have a common right to graze upon the village green and surrounding moorland. This right extends back for hundreds of years.

The village is most famous as the setting of the fictional village of Aidensfield in the *Heartbeat* television series, set in the 1960s. Fans of *Heartbeat* will not be disappointed by a visit to fictional Aidensfield, as many of the series landmarks are recognisable, including the stores,

197

garage/funeral directors, the public house and the railway station. In reality the public house is called the Goathland Hotel, but in the series is the Aidensfield Arms.

[North Yorkshire Moors Railway train crossing the moor (top), LNER teak carriage (bottom left) and *The Green Knight* (bottom right)]

Goathland railway station is on the North Yorkshire Moors Railway, which is a private charitable trust with a number of paid staff but mostly operated by volunteers. The station became Hogsmeade station in *Harry Potter and the Philosopher's Stone* (2001). The railway carries upwards of two hundred and fifty thousand passengers annually and is the second longest preserved line in Britain, linking Grosmont in the north with Pickering in the south. The station (originally known as Goathland Mill) is on the deviation line opened by the North Eastern Railway in 1865 to avoid the cable-worked Beck Hole incline, which was part of the original 1836 Whitby and Pickering Railway route.

It is close to here that the train carrying the Earl and Lady Grantham to Brancaster Castle is seen traversing the moor in the 2015 *Downton Abbey* Christmas special. The locomotive at the head of the train is No. 75029, *The Green Knight* – a British Railways Class 4MT 4-6-0 – built at Swindon in 1954, and so post-dates the series by some decades. The carriages are closer to the correct period being LNER Teak stock designed by Gresley and constructed in the 1930s. However, appearances can be deceptive for all the interiors were actually shot in a Pullman car belonging to the Bluebell Railway in West Sussex (page 191). In fact, only the establishing and background shots are of the North Yorkshire Moors Railway – the cast and crew never visited, so any claim to the location being a *Downton Abbey* one is a little tenuous.

Downton Abbey in Argyll and Bute

Inveraray - Inveraray Castle

[Inveraray Castle doubled as the Duneagle estate in the 'Highlands' of Scotland for the *Downton Abbey* 2012 Christmas special]

The unitary authority of Argyll and Bute, to the north-west of Glasgow, was carved out of the former Strathclyde Region in 1996. It covers most of the county of Argyll and parts of the counties of Bute and Dunbartonshire. The southern islands of the Inner Hebrides, including Islay, Colonsay, Jura, Iona, Mull, Staffa and Tiree, fall within the council area, as of course does the Isle of Bute. In the centre of the mainland area, near the head of Loch Fyne, is the royal burgh of Inveraray, ancestral home of the Dukes of Argyll and former county town of Argyllshire.

In 1747 plans were drawn up by William Adam for a new Inveraray, but so little progress had been made by 1770, that the fifth Duke took control of the project. The Argyll Hotel in Front Street and the Town House, now also a hotel, were designed by William's more famous son John Adam, and many of the other buildings that we see today, including the church, are the work of the celebrated Edinburgh-born architect Robert Mylne. By the end of the eighteenth century Inveraray was a fine example of a Scottish new town, boasting houses for the estate workers, a woollen mill and a pier on the Loch.

The town's coat of arms features a net cast out over the water, in which are five herrings. The motto *Semper Tibi Pendeat Halec* translates roughly as 'May there always be a herring in your net', and the fishing industry is still important to Inveraray, though today it is rivalled by tourism. In 2004 new regulations were introduced requiring drivers to take a break every two hours, and fortuitously for Inveraray the town is a two-hour drive from Glasgow, so both scheduled buses and sightseeing tours are all forced to stop here for at least thirty minutes. There is plenty for visitors to see. The Inveraray Maritime Experience at the pier (recently closed) includes the iron sailing ship *Arctic Penguin* and the last working Clyde Puffer, *Vital Spark*. The Argyll Folk Museum, an original West Highland Township at nearby Auchindrain brings a historic faming village to life. The Georgian Inveraray Jail, now a museum, houses the 'Torture, Death and Damnation' exhibition. The tower of All Saints church, which offers spectacular views over the loch, contains the second-heaviest ring of ten bells in the world. But by far the most impressive building in Inveraray, and the one of most interest to *Downton Abbey* fans, is the castle itself, the seat of the Dukes of Argyll.

The Earls and Marquesses of Argyll lived for nearly three centuries in what was originally a simple laird's tower, surrounded by a few houses, but in the early 1700s the 2nd Duke commissioned Sir John Vanbrugh, architect of Blenheim Palace and Castle Howard, to design a residence more fitting for one of Scotland's most important families. Vanbrugh's plan for a fairly basic castle around a courtyard, four-square, with four corner towers, each with a conical cap, was never built, but it inspired the design that was later built, to the orders of the 2nd Duke's brother and successor. The foundation stone was laid in 1746, and the building that resulted was a truly modern, baroque, Palladian and Gothic-style mansion, architecturally ahead of its time. The architects, Roger Morris and William Adam, both died before work was completed in 1789, and the final stages were supervised by Adam's sons Robert and John. The castle remained largely unchanged until 1877, when fire broke out, causing such damage that the 8th Duke and his family moved to their other house at Rosneath while restoration work took place. The architect this time was Anthony Salvin, who, as well as repairing the fire damage, also proposed the building of a baronial wing. Nothing came of this plan, though Salvin's suggestion for the addition of conical roofs on the corner towers, as in Vanbrugh's original design, was carried out. In 1975 a second, equally devastating fire destroyed the top floor of the castle, along with pictures and furniture stored there. For some months the 12th Duke and his family lived in the castle basement with no electricity or running water, working all hours to restore the building. Despite its neo-gothic exterior, Inveraray Castle is really a classic Georgian mansion on a grand scale, and undoubtedly one of the great treasures of Scotland.

[The bridge where the Granthams are greeted when they arrive, and also where Lady Rose MacClare is caught smoking under one of the arches by Bates and Anna on their post-prandial stroll]

Various parts of the castle were used for the 2012 Christmas special of *Downton Abbey*, entitled *A Journey to the Highlands*. We see the Earl of Grantham and his family arriving at Duneagle, to be greeted on the doubled-arched bridge by the Flintshires, who take them to the Armoury Hall (by the garden entrance, rather than the main entrance).

203

**[The magnificent State Dining Room complete with French
style chairs, which were actually made in the castle
by two Edinburgh craftsmen]**

After the visitors have dressed, it is time for dinner in the State Dining
Room though when Lord Grantham says, "How marvellous!" he is

referring to the piper rather than the magnificent room, which was constructed in 1770 to a design by Robert Mylne. The plasterwork alone took two years to finish. The highly decorated ceiling was cast in London by John Papworth, and the cornice and frieze were created in Scotland by John Clayton. During the dinner conversation we catch a glimpse of the spectacular and intricate silver gilt ship table decorations. They are called 'nefs' and were manufactured in Germany in the 19th century. Although it is not discernable on the television, the sails are engraved with the Argyll coat of arms.

After dinner on the second night, at which Michael Gregson the magazine editor is present, there is a charming scene in which we see Bates and Anna walking under the bridge, where they find Lady Rose having a cigarette. Very soon Lady Flintshire is heard calling for her daughter from above, but not before Bates has given her a mint to disguise the smell on her breath.

[The spot where Bates and Anna take their picnic]

On the following day, while the male Granthams go shooting, Bates and Anna (who seem to be having a holiday of their own), are seen having a romantic picnic beside the large bridge over the River Aray, to the north of the castle. "Is there anything to drink?" asks Bates. "There certainly is," replies Anna, producing a bottle of beer. Bates considers this 'racy', and it does at least seem unlikely that the servants would have been allowed alcohol, when presumably they would shortly be back on duty at the castle.

[The perfect spot for a picnic or salmon fishing]

At the same time the female Granthams (who are later joined by the Earl and Shrimpy Flintshire) are having their own, rather more formal picnic, about a mile from the castle and just off Old Military Road (A83), beside Dubh Loch – which gives its name to Loch Dhu whisky. The skies look decidedly too dark for a picnic, even for one under canvas. As ever, it is left to the Dowager Countess, who is seen flicking away the midges (which were a problem for the actors during the filming by the water) to come up with the best comment of the day, when she says, "That is the thing about nature: there is so much of it."

The scene showing Matthew Crawley and Michael Gregson fishing for salmon was also shot near Dubh Loch, by the bridge on the River Shira. It is here that Gregson pours out his heart as he complains that he is "prevented from divorcing a woman who doesn't even know who I am.

Does the law expect me to have no life at all until I die?" At first Crawley is not sympathetic, pointing out that all Gregson is offering Lady Edith is a "job as your mistress". However, once he realises that Gregson is in love with her, Crawley softens his approach, saying that Gregson has been "… misled by our surroundings. We're not in a novel by Walter Scott." But though he agrees that the editor's position is tragic, he is unwilling to let Lady Edith "slide into a life of scandal", and suggests that he uses the impending Ghillies' ball to "say a proper goodbye".

[The landing where Wilkins asks O'Brien to see to Lady Flintshire's hair, and the staircase where Lady Rose shows off the latest fashion, much to her mother's disapproval, prior to the Ghillies' Ball]

Other key scenes take place just before the Ghillies' Ball (which is held in the castle but not actually filmed there). Things get off to an awkward start when Lady Rose appears on the staircase (actually the one on the private side of the castle, not open to the public) wearing the latest fashion, which her mother demands she changes out of immediately. An argument ensues, in which Shrimpy stands up for his daughter and entreats his wife to "stop making everyone so unhappy". This is not before Lady Flintshire calls her daughter a slut, prompting the Dowager Countess to remark, "Heavens! That's not a word you often hear among the heather." Later on, observing the obvious rift between mother and daughter, she comments, "Poor soul! It's bad enough parenting a child when you like each other."

[The Armoury Hall]

Finally, note should be made of the Armoury Hall, which is seen in several passing shots. Developed from Vanbrugh's original sketch from 1720, the hall soars to 21 metres in height, the highest ceiling in Scotland, and is well lit, with the light coming in different directions through the arches. It is the perfect setting for the arms displayed here in decorative patterns on the walls. There are 16th and 17th century pole-arms, roundels of Brown Bess muskets dating from about 1740, and spandrels of muskets alternating with Lochaber axes from the mid-Victorian period. One of the display tables contains the belt and sporran worn by Rob Roy.

Inveraray Castle is open to the public every day from the beginning of April until the end of October. Tours of the private apartments are available by prior arrangement. General adult admission costs around £10 for entry to both the castle and gardens, and the normal discounts are available for children, families, groups and senior citizens. The castle is one of the essential attractions of Scotland, even for those with no interest in the *Downton Abbey* connections. Prospective visitors should check the castle web site (www.inveraray-castle.com) for information on special events.

INVERARAY CASTLE

Opening Times

1st April – 31st October

7 days 10am – 5.45pm

Last admission 5pm

• Gift Shop • Tearoom

www.bowfest.co.uk
w: www.inveraray-castle.com
e: enquiries@inveraray-castle.com
t: 01499 302203

DOWNTON ABBEY ON LOCATION MAPS

The following maps show the relative positions of the various locations covered in the text. The associated tables give both the type of place, according to the defined symbols below, along with the page number in brackets and postcode for that location. It is hoped that the maps will help readers in planning their own visits to these places of *Downton Abbey* interest.

Key to Symbols

	Building (large or important)		Building (general place or structure)		Church (religious establishment)
	Hotel or Restaurant		Military Establishment		Natural Feature (park or garden)
	Tourist Attraction (museum)		Transport Related		

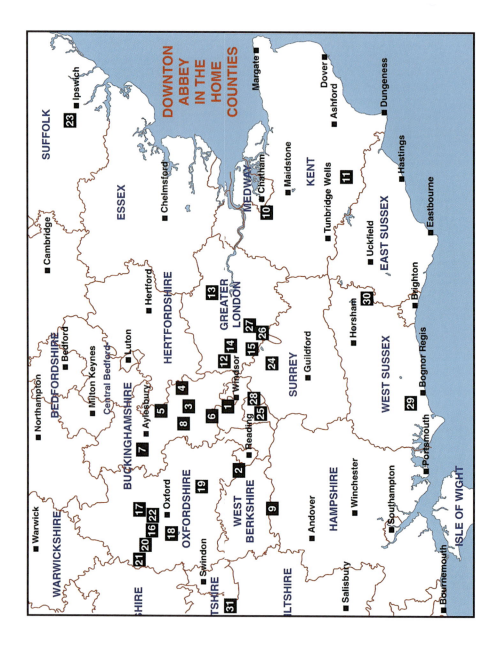

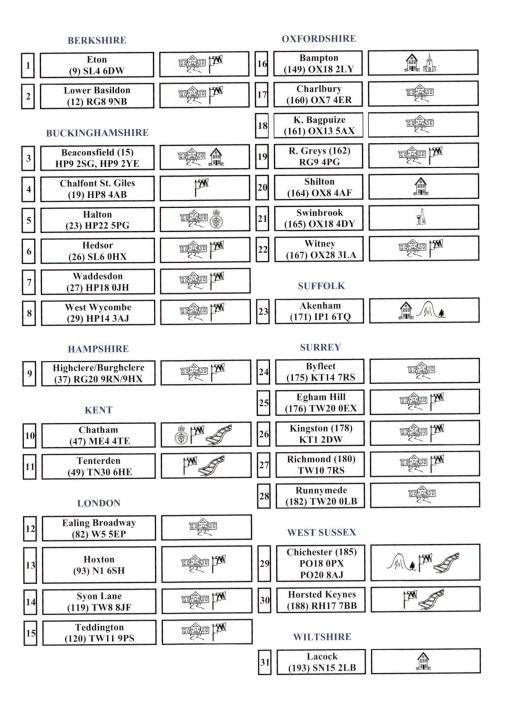

BERKSHIRE

| 1 | Eton (9) SL4 6DW |
| 2 | Lower Basildon (12) RG8 9NB |

BUCKINGHAMSHIRE

3	Beaconsfield (15) HP9 2SG, HP9 2YE
4	Chalfont St. Giles (19) HP8 4AB
5	Halton (23) HP22 5PG
6	Hedsor (26) SL6 0HX
7	Waddesdon (27) HP18 0JH
8	West Wycombe (29) HP14 3AJ

HAMPSHIRE

| 9 | Highclere/Burghclere (37) RG20 9RN/9HX |

KENT

| 10 | Chatham (47) ME4 4TE |
| 11 | Tenterden (49) TN30 6HE |

LONDON

12	Ealing Broadway (82) W5 5EP
13	Hoxton (93) N1 6SH
14	Syon Lane (119) TW8 8JF
15	Teddington (120) TW11 9PS

OXFORDSHIRE

16	Bampton (149) OX18 2LY
17	Charlbury (160) OX7 4ER
18	K. Bagpuize (161) OX13 5AX
19	R. Greys (162) RG9 4PG
20	Shilton (164) OX8 4AF
21	Swinbrook (165) OX18 4DY
22	Witney (167) OX28 3LA

SUFFOLK

| 23 | Akenham (171) IP1 6TQ |

SURREY

24	Byfleet (175) KT14 7RS
25	Egham Hill (176) TW20 0EX
26	Kingston (178) KT1 2DW
27	Richmond (180) TW10 7RS
28	Runnymede (182) TW20 0LB

WEST SUSSEX

| 29 | Chichester (185) PO18 0PX PO20 8AJ |
| 30 | Horsted Keynes (188) RH17 7BB |

WILTSHIRE

| 31 | Lacock (193) SN15 2LB |

213

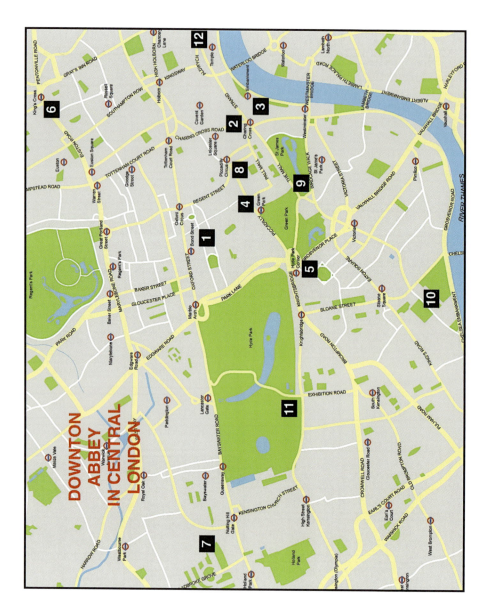

1	**Bond Street** (71) **W1K 4ER**	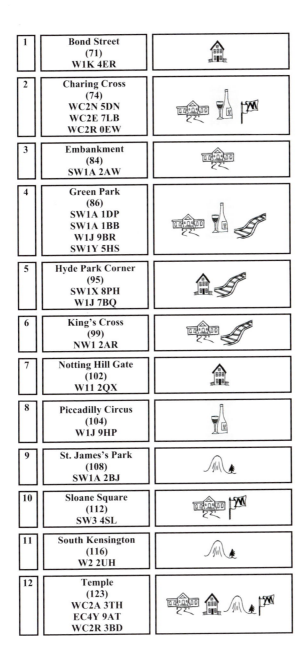
2	**Charing Cross** (74) **WC2N 5DN** **WC2E 7LB** **WC2R 0EW**	
3	**Embankment** (84) **SW1A 2AW**	
4	**Green Park** (86) **SW1A 1DP** **SW1A 1BB** **W1J 9BR** **SW1Y 5HS**	
5	**Hyde Park Corner** (95) **SW1X 8PH** **W1J 7BQ**	
6	**King's Cross** (99) **NW1 2AR**	
7	**Notting Hill Gate** (102) **W11 2QX**	
8	**Piccadilly Circus** (104) **W1J 9HP**	
9	**St. James's Park** (108) **SW1A 2BJ**	
10	**Sloane Square** (112) **SW3 4SL**	
11	**South Kensington** (116) **W2 2UH**	
12	**Temple** (123) **WC2A 3TH** **EC4Y 9AT** **WC2R 3BD**	

215

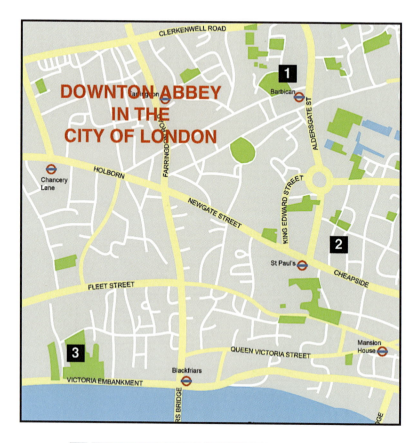

DOWNTON ABBEY IN THE CITY OF LONDON

1		Barbican (63) EC1M 6AN	
3		St. Paul's (110) EC2V 6BN	
3		Temple (123) WC2A 3TH EC4Y 9AT WC2R 3BD	

1	Alnwick (137) NE66 1YU	
2	Beamish (33) DH9 0RG	
3	Goathland (197) YO22 5NF	
4	Lincoln (53) LN1 3AA	

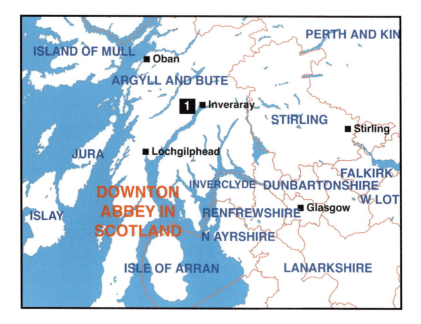

| 1 | Inveraray
(201)
PA32 8XE | |

PLACES INDEX

Transport Related

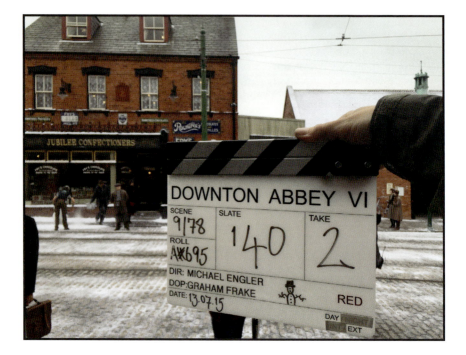

ACKNOWLEDGMENTS

The authors and publisher are delighted to be able to thank all those who have supported this publication from its inception.

With the exception of those listed here all photographs in this book were either already in the public domain, or were taken by the authors. Our thanks is given to all those who have graciously given permission for their photographs to be used in this book: Alnwick Castle and Sean Elliott (pages 137-142, 144 & 146), Beamish Museum (pages 33, 35 & 222), Michael Blackburn (pages 7, 189-190 and back cover), Des Blenkinsopp (page 161), Chiltern Open Air Museum (pages 21 & 22), Peter Dazeley (pages 134-135), Reinhard Dietrich (page 198 top), Paul Faraday (page 180), Gryffindor (page 89), Derek Harper (page 194 top), Inveraray Castle (pages 204 & 207), Kelly (page 12), D. G. Kent (page 191), Langdon Down Centre (page 121), Barry Lewis (page 198 bottom left), Lincoln Castle (page 53), Magnus Manske (pages 119 & 198 bottom left), David Merrett (page 185), Clive Nicholson (page 145), Philafrenzy (page 92 bottom), Elisa Rolle (page 124 bottom), Royal Holloway, University of London (pages 177-178), Rudolph Schuba (page 75), Crosbie Smith (p160), David Stokes (page 187), Joan Street (page 28) and Chris Talbot (page 46).

Special thanks goes to Roger Johnson for his editing and proof reading skills. In alphabetical order the following are also thanked for their generous time, advice and expertise: Lesley Alabaf (Langdon Down Centre), the Duke of Argyll (Inveraray Castle), Eleanor Argyll (Inveraray Castle), Mr. David Bauer, Candice Bauval (Highclere Castle), Rachel Bellon (The Bulldog Trust), Mr. Michael Blackburn (Bluebell Railway), the Countess of Carnarvon (Highclere Castle), Christie Cannings (Photoshot), Patrizia Cox (The Savile Club), Serena Hedley-Dent (Eton College), Jenefer Farncombe (Hall Barn), Nicoletta Falotico (Savini at Criterion), Mr. André Freeman (Kent & East Sussex Railway), Madeleine Hawkins (Lincoln Castle), Rebecca Hone (The Bulldog Trust), Richard McCrow (The Goldsmiths' Company), Harriet O'Neal (Royal Holloway, University of London), John Patrick (Inveraray Castle), Stephanie Papadopoulos (No. 4 Hamilton Place), Stuart Richardson (Alnwick Castle), Sue Shave (Chiltern Open Air Museum), Colin Shone (Cogges Heritage Enterprises), Olivia Telfer (Alnwick Castle), Jacki Winstanley (Beamish Museum) and Jane Young (Inveraray Castle).

Finally, at a corporate level gratitude goes to Carnival Film and Television Limited, Universal Studios, Universal Pictures (UK) Limited and Julian Fellowes for creating *Downton Abbey* without them this publication would not exist.

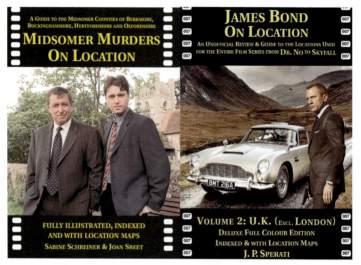